FORCE REDUCTION

MARINE AND ARMY DRAWDOWNS EXAMINED, IN BRIEF

MILITARY AND VETERAN ISSUES

Additional books in this series can be found on Nova's website
under the Series tab.

Additional e-books in this series can be found on Nova's website
under the e-book tab.

MILITARY AND VETERAN ISSUES

FORCE REDUCTION

MARINE AND ARMY DRAWDOWNS EXAMINED, IN BRIEF

GEOFFREY HOPKINS
EDITOR

New York

Library of Congress Cataloging-in-Publication Data

ISBN: 978-1-63117-586-2

Published by Nova Science Publishers, Inc. † *New York*

CONTENTS

PREFACE

This book examines the drawdown of the Marine Corps, as well as the force structure initiatives, roles and missions, and the restructuring of the Marine Corps.

Chapter 1 – The Marine Corps characterizes itself as a crisis response expeditionary force which is task organized and able to conduct operations across the entire spectrum of military operations. The Corps is a "middleweight force" that is designed to fill the void in our Nation's defense structure between light Special Operations Forces (SOF) and heavier conventional units. The Marines' missions are codified in U.S. Code, Title 10, Section 5063, United States Marine Corps: Composition and Functions, and marines are the nation's primary amphibious force, capable of conducting amphibious assault operations in both permissive and non-permissive environments. Marine operational forces are organized for specific tasks and consist of four elements; a command element; a ground combat element; an aviation element; and a logistics combat element. There are four types of Marine Air Ground Task Forces (MAGTFs): the Marine Expeditionary Force (MEF); the Marine Expeditionary Brigade (MEB); the Marine Expeditionary Unit (MEU); and the Special Purpose MAGTF.

A number of decisions pertaining to national security strategy, force structure, and declining defense budgets have resulted in a drawdown of the active Marine Corps from 202,000 in 2011 to 174,000 by 2017. Some believe that if sequestration continues, the Marines could be compelled to draw down to a force of 150,000 Marines—a strength level Marine Corps leadership has characterized as unviable to execute our current defense strategy.

The Marines have instituted a number of force shaping programs to reach the 174,000 endstrength. They believe this force level can be achieved through natural attrition as well as voluntary separation programs where Marines who leave the service early can receive financial compensation. Officials caution that if the Marines are required to drawdown to 150,000, involuntary separation programs might need to be enacted.

The Marines have instituted a number of force structure initiatives including creating Special Purpose MAGTFs - Crisis Response (SPMAGTF-CR) to respond to a variety of regional crises, including attacks on U.S. diplomatic facilities and personnel. In the wake of the September 11, 2012, Benghazi attack, Congress authorized 1,000 additional Marine security guards beginning FY 2014. In response, the Marines are in the process of expanding their Marine Corps Embassy Security Group. The Marine Corps Special Operations Command (MARSOC) is also regionally-aligning its operational units and taking steps to begin deploying small MARSOC teams with MEUs.

A sampling of academic discussions focusing on the Marine Corps of the future suggests the Marines and Special Operations Forces (SOF) could be given the lead responsibility for worldwide ground engagement. Another proposal suggests that Marines should operate in small, decentralized units and that the Marines' focus could shift to company and battalion-sized units, the so-called "sweet spot" for joint ground forces. Others contend that more Marine major war fighting units, such as armor, be moved into the Marine Corps Reserves and that Marine Aviation should be reorganized.

A potential issue for Congress includes should the Marines be given the leading role in the Pacific and should their primary focus be crisis response? Other possible issues for examination include how much amphibious assault capability does the Marine Corps need; should MEUs be reorganized; and should more of the Marines' major warfighting capability be placed in the Reserves?

Chapter 2 – On January 26, 2012, senior DOD leadership unveiled a new defense strategy based on a review of potential future security challenges, current defense strategy, and budgetary constraints. This new strategy envisions a smaller, leaner Army that is agile, flexible, rapidly deployable, and technologically advanced. This strategy will rebalance the Army's global posture and presence, emphasizing where potential problems are likely to arise, such as the Asia-Pacific region and the Middle East.

As part of the Administration's original proposal, two armored brigade combat teams (ABCTs) in Europe were to be eliminated out of a total of eight BCTs that would be cut from Active Army force structure. The Army had originally stated that it might cut more than eight BCTs from the Army's current 44 Active BCTs. Army endstrength would go from 570,000 in 2010 to

490,000 by the end of 2017. As part of this reduction, the Army would no longer be sized to conduct large-scale, protracted stability operations but would continue to be a full-spectrum force capable of addressing a wide range of national security challenges. The Army National Guard and Army Reserves were not targeted for significant cuts. Army leadership stated the impending decrease in Active Duty Army force structure would place an even greater reliance on the National Guard and Reserves.

On June 25, 2013, the Army announced it would cut 12 BCTs from the Active Army as well as a number of unspecified support and headquarters units. As part of this initiative, infantry and armored BCTs would receive a third maneuver battalion plus additional engineering and fires capabilities. In addition, National Guard BCTs would also be restructured in a similar fashion. Due to the impact of sequestration, the Army also decided to accelerate the Active Army drawdown to 490,000 soldiers by two years—these cuts would now need to be completed by the end of 2015. In an effort to reduce costs, the Army also announced that it would examine cutting all two-star and higher headquarters staffs by 25%—a figure that includes soldiers, Army civilians, and contractors.

There will likely be a human dimension of the Army's drawdown. Troops have received an unprecedented level of support from the American public, and those soldiers leaving the service—voluntarily and perhaps involuntarily—might have strong personal feelings about leaving the Army and their comrades after multiple deployments to combat zones. The Army drawdown will likely be achieved in large degree by controlling accessions (i.e., the number of people allowed to join the Army). If limiting accessions is not enough to achieve the desired endstrength targets, the Army can employ a variety of involuntary and voluntary drawdown tools authorized by Congress, such as Selective Early Retirement Boards (SERBs) and Reduction-inForce (RIF). Voluntary tools that the Army might use include the Voluntary Retirement Incentive, the Voluntary Separation Incentive, Special Separation Bonuses, Temporary Early Retirement Authority, the Voluntary Early Release/Retirement Program, and Early Outs.

The Administration's proposals to drawdown and restructure the Army raise some potential issues for congressional consideration. These questions include the potential impacts of accelerating the Army's drawdown by two years and whether the current Active Component/Reserve Component force mix should be reexamined.

Chapter 3 – John Carpenter, film director of horror movies such as *Halloween*, was once asked what he thought it was that scared theater audiences the most. His answer was simple: "Uncertainty." Carpenter understood that not knowing what will happen next often produces more anxiety and angst than actual traumatic events. As anyone who has sat on the edge of their chair during thrillers such as *Psycho* or *Jaws* understands, it's the apprehension and dread resulting from uncertainty that exacts the most psychological toll from viewers.

In: Force Reduction
Editor: Geoffrey Hopkins

ISBN: 978-1-63117-586-2
© 2014 Nova Science Publishers, Inc.

Chapter 1

MARINE CORPS DRAWDOWN, FORCE STRUCTURE INITIATIVES, AND ROLES AND MISSIONS: BACKGROUND AND ISSUES FOR CONGRESS[*]

Andrew Feickert

SUMMARY

The Marine Corps characterizes itself as a crisis response expeditionary force which is task organized and able to conduct operations across the entire spectrum of military operations. The Corps is a "middleweight force" that is designed to fill the void in our Nation's defense structure between light Special Operations Forces (SOF) and heavier conventional units. The Marines' missions are codified in U.S. Code, Title 10, Section 5063, United States Marine Corps: Composition and Functions, and marines are the nation's primary amphibious force, capable of conducting amphibious assault operations in both permissive and non-permissive environments. Marine operational forces are organized for specific tasks and consist of four elements; a command element; a ground combat element; an aviation element; and a logistics

---

[*] This is an edited, reformatted and augmented version of a Congressional Research Service publication, CRS Report for Congress R43355, from www.crs.gov, prepared for Members and Committees of Congress, dated January 9, 2014.

combat element. There are four types of Marine Air Ground Task Forces (MAGTFs): the Marine Expeditionary Force (MEF); the Marine Expeditionary Brigade (MEB); the Marine Expeditionary Unit (MEU); and the Special Purpose MAGTF.

A number of decisions pertaining to national security strategy, force structure, and declining defense budgets have resulted in a drawdown of the active Marine Corps from 202,000 in 2011 to 174,000 by 2017. Some believe that if sequestration continues, the Marines could be compelled to draw down to a force of 150,000 Marines—a strength level Marine Corps leadership has characterized as unviable to execute our current defense strategy.

The Marines have instituted a number of force shaping programs to reach the 174,000 endstrength. They believe this force level can be achieved through natural attrition as well as voluntary separation programs where Marines who leave the service early can receive financial compensation. Officials caution that if the Marines are required to drawdown to 150,000, involuntary separation programs might need to be enacted.

The Marines have instituted a number of force structure initiatives including creating Special Purpose MAGTFs - Crisis Response (SPMAGTF-CR) to respond to a variety of regional crises, including attacks on U.S. diplomatic facilities and personnel. In the wake of the September 11, 2012, Benghazi attack, Congress authorized 1,000 additional Marine security guards beginning FY 2014. In response, the Marines are in the process of expanding their Marine Corps Embassy Security Group. The Marine Corps Special Operations Command (MARSOC) is also regionally-aligning its operational units and taking steps to begin deploying small MARSOC teams with MEUs.

A sampling of academic discussions focusing on the Marine Corps of the future suggests the Marines and Special Operations Forces (SOF) could be given the lead responsibility for worldwide ground engagement. Another proposal suggests that Marines should operate in small, decentralized units and that the Marines' focus could shift to company and battalion-sized units, the so-called "sweet spot" for joint ground forces. Others contend that more Marine major war fighting units, such as armor, be moved into the Marine Corps Reserves and that Marine Aviation should be reorganized.

A potential issue for Congress includes should the Marines be given the leading role in the Pacific and should their primary focus be crisis response? Other possible issues for examination include how much amphibious assault capability does the Marine Corps need; should MEUs be reorganized; and should more of the Marines' major warfighting capability be placed in the Reserves?

IMPORTANCE TO CONGRESS

The Administration's proposal to reduce the size of the Marine Corps has national security implications that Congress may consider as part of its oversight and authorizations and appropriations roles. In terms of size of the force, Congress sets the endstrength[1] for both the active Marine Corps and the Marine Corps Reserve. Congress also authorizes and appropriates funds needed for Marine force structure initiatives, training exercises, equipment, basing, and infrastructure, as well as the various manpower management tools which could be used to drawdown the force. Administration decisions about the recommended size and basing of the Marine Corps can have a significant impact on Marine bases in a Member's district or state, which can also have economic ramifications for communities near affected bases. The Administration's downsizing and force structure proposals also can have a significant impact on local and state defense-related industries. Lastly, Marines and their families who might be affected by the Administration's decisions constitute a unique element of Members' constituencies.

BACKGROUND

Marine Corps Roles and Missions

According to the Marine Corps:

> The Marine Corps is a crisis response expeditionary force which is task organized and able to conduct operations across the entire spectrum of military operations. Fundamentally, the Corps is a "middleweight force" that fills the void in our Nation's defense structure between light Special Operations Forces (SOF) and heavier conventional units. The Corps provides scalable and adaptive forces that complement the lighter and heavier forces.[2]

The Marines serve in a variety of capacities but are perhaps best known as America's amphibious force, with various Marine units embarked on U.S. Navy ships that patrol oceans, littorals, and maritime choke points. The Marines' missions are codified in U.S. Code, Title 10, Section 5063, *United States Marine Corps: Composition and Functions*, dated January 3, 2012, which states:

The Marine Corps shall be organized, trained, and equipped to provide fleet marine forces of combined arms, together with supporting air components, for service with the fleet in the seizure or defense of advanced naval bases and for the conduct of such land operations as may be essential to the prosecution of a naval campaign. In addition, the Marine Corps shall provide detachments and organizations for service on armed vessels of the Navy, shall provide security detachments for the protection of naval property at naval stations and bases, and shall perform such other duties as the President may direct. However, these additional duties may not detract from or interfere with the operations for which the Marine Corps is primarily organized.

(b) The Marine Corps shall develop, in coordination with the Army and the Air Force, those phases of amphibious operations that pertain to the tactics, technique, and equipment used by landing forces.[3]

The Marines two fundamental core missions are assuring *littoral access* and conducting highly complex and difficult *crisis response* operations.[4] In addition to these missions, the Marine Corps has also provided security for overseas U.S. diplomatic missions since 1799 and the Marine Corps Embassy Security Group (MCESG) is responsible for the internal security of these facilities worldwide.[5] In addition to the aforementioned missions, the Marines also have nuclear, chemical, biological incident response responsibilities, conduct security cooperation activities, and are responsible for presidential security and transportation missions.

Marine Corps Reserve

The Marine Corps Reserve was established in 1916 and provides trained units and individual Marines that can be mobilized for active duty in time of war, national emergency or contingency operations. The endstrength of the Marine Corps Reserves was at 39,600 Marines at the end of September 2013.[6] The 4th Marine Division headquartered in New Orleans, LA is the Marine Corps Reserve division and consists of Marine infantry regiments, an aircraft wing, a logistics group, tank units, force reconnaissance, units, and civil affairs units to name but a few of the organizations resident in the Marine Corps Reserve. The Marine Corps Reserve saw active service in Operation Iraqi Freedom and Operation Enduring Freedom in Afghanistan and continues to participate in operations world-wide.

Size of Selected Marine Corps Units[7]
Marine Infantry Squad: 13 Marine Infantry Platoon: 43 Marine Infantry Company: 182 Marine Infantry Battalion: 963 personnel Marine Infantry Regiment: 3,129 personnel Marine Expeditionary Unit (MEU): Approximately 2,200 personnel Marine Expeditionary Brigade (MEB): 14,000 – 17,000 personnel Marine Expeditionary Force (MEF): 40,000 – 80,000 personnel

How the Marines Organize their Operational Forces[8]

Marine Air-Ground Task Force (MAGTF)

The MAGTF is the Marine Corps primary organizational construct for conducting military operations. They range in size from a few hundred to many thousands of Marines and can be embarked on amphibious ships but can also be deployed by other means. They are organized for specific tasks and are comprised of four deployable elements:

- The *Command Element (CE)* which contains the MAGTF headquarters as well as operations, intelligence, logistics, communications, and administrative support.
- The *Ground Combat Element (GCE)* which includes infantry, artillery, reconnaissance, armor, light armor, assault amphibian, engineer, and other forces as needed. In the case of non-combat missions, other types of Marine units can be substituted for combat units.
- The *Aviation Combat Element (ACE)* is comprised of a variety of aircraft and support units needed to support MAGTF operations. Types of support include assault support, anti-air warfare, offensive air support, electronic warfare, control of aircraft and missiles, and reconnaissance. The ACE is also capable of providing support for humanitarian relief and disaster relief operations.
- The *Logistics Combat Element (LCE)* is organized to provide a full range of combat logistics functions and capabilities needed to sustain the MAGTF.

Types of MAGTFs

There are four types of MAGTFs: the Marine Expeditionary Force (MEF); the Marine Expeditionary Brigade (MEB); the Marine Expeditionary Unit (MEU); and the Special Purpose MAGTF.

Marine Expeditionary Force (MEF)

The MEF is the principal warfighting organization for large crises or contingencies. During the 2003 invasion of Iraq (Operation Iraqi Freedom) the 1st MEF was the major Marine Corps unit deployed as part of the U.S. invasion force. The MEF is normally commanded by a lieutenant general, consists of approximately 40,000 to 80,000 personnel, and can range in size from one division and an air wing to multiple divisions and air wings supported by one or more logistics groups. The Marine Corps is organized with three standing MEFs in both peacetime and wartime, with each comprised of a Marine division, aircraft wing, and logistics group. The 1st MEF is located at bases in California and Arizona; the 2nd MEF at bases in North Carolina and South Carolina; and the 3rd MEF at bases in Okinawa, mainland Japan, and Hawaii with future plans for bases in Guam and Australia.[9] As previously noted, the Marine Corps Reserve 4th MEF is headquartered out of New Orleans, LA.

Marine Expeditionary Brigade (MEB)

The MEB is a mid-sized MAGTF which consists of from 14,000 to 17,000 personnel and is normally commanded by a brigadier general. The MEB is scalable and can respond to a full range of contingencies. The MEB, when at sea, is normally embarked on 17 amphibious ships and carries with it 30 days of supplies, meaning it can operate ashore for 30 days before it requires resupply. The MEB is normally comprised of a reinforced infantry regiment, a composite Marine Aircraft Group, and a Combat Logistics Regiment. MEBs do not have permanently assigned units but instead maintain a habitual relationship with subordinate units through planning and exercises.

Marine Expeditionary Unit (MEU)

MEUs are embarked on Amphibious Readiness Groups (ARG)[10] and operate on a continuous basis in the areas of responsibility of certain Geographic Combatant Commanders. A MEU is commanded by a Colonel, can include up to about 2,200 Marines, and deploys with 15 days of accompanying supplies. Before a MEU deploys, it undergoes an intensive six month training program and the MEU is then evaluated and certified for deployment. The types of operations that a MEU is trained and equip to conduct include:

- Amphibious assault landing;
- Amphibious raid;[11]
- Small boat raid (in selected MEUs only);
- Maritime interception operations;
- Advance force operations;
- Noncombatant evacuation operations;
- Humanitarian assistance;
- Stability operations;
- Tactical recovery of aircraft and personnel;
- Joint and combined operations;
- Aviation operations from expeditionary sites;
- Theater security cooperation activities; and
- Airfield and port seizures.

Special Purpose MAGTF (SPMAGTF)

A SPMAGTF is organized to accomplish a specific mission, operation, or regionally-focused activity. They can be organized, trained, and equipped to conduct a variety of operations ranging from peacetime missions, training exercises, and responses to contingencies and crises. Because of unique mission requirements, there is no set size or structure associated with SPMAGTFs.

Decisions Impacting Marine Corps Size and Force Structure

January 6, 2011, News Briefing with Secretary of Defense Gates and Chairman of the Joint Chiefs of Staff Admiral Mullen[12]

On January 6, 2011, then Secretary of Defense Robert Gates and then Chairman of the Joint Chiefs of Staff Admiral Mike Mullen held a news briefing "announcing a number of decisions and measures that mark the next major step in this department's reform agenda." These decisions and measures, largely taken in response to fiscal pressures, involved a variety of cross-service actions, including consolidating and eliminating headquarters and organizations, modifying or eliminating weapon systems programs, and force reductions. During this briefing, it was announced the Marines would drawdown between 15,000 and 20,000 Marines - depending on the recommendations of a Marine Force Structure Review Group - with a goal of eventually reducing the Marine Corps to 175,000.

March 14, 2011, Report of the 2010 Marine Corps Force Structure Review Group[13]

In March 2011, the Marines released the results of a force structure review focused on the post-Afghanistan Marine Corps, which was intended to preserve capabilities developed since September 11, 2001; expand on engagement efforts; respond to crisis; and still be capable of projecting power to respond to the most dangerous threats to the nation. In order to achieve this desired end state, the Marines stated they would accept a degree of risk by reducing the active component capacity "for conducting multiple, major sustained operations ashore, relying on an operationalized reserve component to mitigate the risk."[14] Key recommendations from the review included:

- Reduce the endstrength of the active component from 202,000 to approximately 186,800 *following the completion of Marine operations in Afghanistan*;
- Resource five regionally-focused MEB command elements, with habitually aligned subordinate elements in order to improve effectiveness and responsiveness;
- Reduce infantry battalions from 27 to 24;
- Reduce artillery battalions from 11 to 9;
- Reduce flying squadrons from 70 to 61;
- Reorganize Marine logistics groups; and
- Increase Marine Corps Special Operations Command (MARSOC)[15] by more than 1,000 Marines.

January 26, 2012, Administration Major Budget Decision Briefing[16]

On January 26, 2012, senior DOD leaders unveiled a new defense strategy, based on a review of the defense strategy at the time and budgetary constraints. This new strategy envisioned:

- A smaller, leaner military that is agile, flexible, rapidly deployable, and technologically advanced;

- Rebalancing global posture and presence, emphasizing where potential problems are likely to arise, such as the Asia-Pacific region[17] and the Middle East;
- Maintaining presence elsewhere in the world (Europe, Africa, and Latin America), using innovative partnerships, strengthening key alliances, and developing new partnerships;
- Being able to quickly confront and defeat aggression from any adversary anytime, anyplace; and
- Protecting and prioritizing key investments in technology and new capabilities as well as the capacity to grow, adapt, mobilize, and surge when needed.

During this briefing, a number of decisions related to the Marine Corps were announced, including:

- The Marines would be a middleweight expeditionary force with reinvigorated amphibious capabilities;
- The Active Marine Corps would decrease from 202,000 Marines to 182,000 over five years (2017);
- There would be no decrease in the size of the Marine Corps Reserve;
- This new strategy envisioned a Navy and Marine Corps that was postured forward; and
- The Marines would sustain their level of presence in the Pacific and enhance their presence by partnering with Australia and others, such as the Philippines.

2013 Strategic Choices and Management Review (SCMR)[18]

In April 2013, Secretary of Defense Chuck Hagel announced that DOD would conduct a Strategic Choices and Management Review (SCMR) to help insure that the Defense Department would be prepared to face what he called "unprecedented budget uncertainty."[19] The three stated specific objectives of the SCMR were to:

- Help DOD prepare for how to deal with sequestration if it continues into FY 2014;
- Inform the fiscal guidance given to the Services for their FY 2015 through FY 2019 budget plans; and

- Anchor the upcoming Quadrennial Defense Review (QDR) which plans to assess our defense strategy in light of new fiscal realities and the many threats and complexities and uncertainties of this new century.

In a July 31, 2013, statement, Secretary Hagel, commenting on the results of the SCMR, described two strategic approaches to reducing force structure and modernization that would be used to inform planning for sequester-level cuts. These approaches would trade off capacity—measured in Army brigades, Navy ships, Air Force squadrons, and Marine battalions—and capability, i.e., the ability to modernize weapon systems and maintain the military's technological edge. In the approach that would trade away size for high-end capacity, Secretary Hagel suggested that the Marines would draw down from 182,000 to between 150,000 and 175,000 active Marines.

2014 Quadrennial Defense Review (QDR)[20]

The Quadrennial Defense Review or QDR, "a congressionally mandated[21] review of national defense strategy, force structure, modernization plans, infrastructure, budget plans, and other elements of defense strategy," is presently underway and is due to Congress in February 2014.

The 2014 QDR will likely have very specific guidance as to Marine Corps force size and organization, among other things, and results from the 2013 SCMR will likely heavily influence decisions coming from the 2014 QDR. Congress is also required to conduct an independent review of the QDR's force structure and resource requirements and submit an assessment to the congressional defense committees no later than May 2014.

Current Marine Force Posture[22]

As of the end of October 2013, the Marines had approximately 22,200 Marines deployed with about 14,000 on operations and about 6,700 Marines afloat in support of operations. Marines are also supporting the various combatant commands (less U.S. Special Operations Command) as follows (all force levels approximate):

- U.S. Northern Command: 50
- U.S. European Command: 2,700
- Afghanistan: 8,000

- Other U.S. Central Command: 3,650
- U.S. Southern Command: 100
- U.S. Africa Command: 1,100
- U.S. Pacific Command: 6,600

The Marines also have three MEUs embarked—the 26th MEU in the U.S. European Command region; the 13th MEU in the U.S. Central Command Region; and the 31st MEU in the U.S. Pacific Command region.

Current Planned Drawdown Levels

In a November 7, 2013, Senate Armed Services Committee (SASC) hearing on the effects of sequestration, Commandant of the Marine Corps General James Amos testified:

> The President's National Security Strategy is optimized with a Marine Corps of 186.8K. The BCA [Budget Control Act of 2011, P.L. 112-25] forced us to 182.1K. Our examination determined that an end strength of 174K was the best we could do in addressing the operational requirements of steady state deployments, crisis response activities, and potential major combat operations, while preserving institutional health and readiness. As we actively participate in the QDR, this is the force that the Marine Corps will use as the recommended basis for our contribution to the nation's defense. Based on extensive analysis, falling below this force structure number will significantly increase risk in to our steady state security posture, crisis response and major combat operations.[23]

The 174,000 Active Marine Corps endstrength figure cited by General Amos will be the Marines' planning endstrength as the QDR process progresses. While the Marines did not offer specifics about force structure reductions needed to reach the 174,000 active Marine endstrength by 2017, reports suggest that an additional five infantry battalions would be eliminated and, at this force level, the Marines would only be able to respond to one major contingency.[24] Also at this level, any planned growth in the Marine Special Operations Command (MARSOC)[25] would reportedly be frozen and the three-star Marine Expeditionary Force (MEF) headquarters—II MEF from Camp Lejeune, NC—would be absorbed by Marine Forces Command in Norfolk, VA.[26]

As previously noted, Secretary Hagel in discussing the SCMR suggested Marines could draw down from 182,000 to between 175,000 - 150,000 active Marines. Marine officials have reportedly concluded that a 150,000 Marine force would be a "dangerously small force" and "unviable" for accomplishing the Marine's current mission.[27]

FORCE REDUCTION AND SHAPING PROGRAMS

Reportedly, Marine officials believe they can achieve this 174,000 active duty level without having to force Marines out of service before their contracts expire.[28] To date, the drawdown has reportedly been achieved through normal attrition and early out incentives; including premature retirements and cash buyouts which have permitted the service reduce active endstrength by about 5,000 personnel per year.[29] In order to retain key capabilities such as special operations and cyber operations, cuts would primarily come from infantry and artillery battalions and aviation squadrons.

Marine officials suggest, however, if force cuts are accelerated or if the Marines are required to cut to a 150,000 active endstrength, that involuntary measures would need to be taken in addition to voluntary programs currently being used.[30] Some involuntary measures include:

- Ending a "de facto" guarantee of 20 years of service for all enlisted Marines who reach the grade of staff sergeant;
- Convening an early retirement board for senior enlisted Marines;
- Using enlisted retention boards to cut Marines before their contracts expired;
- Ending a 20 year service promise to all Marine officers who make the grade of major; and
- Selective Early Retirement Board for lieutenant colonels and colonels.

FORCE STRUCTURE INITIATIVES

As the Marines drawdown, a number of force structure-related initiatives are underway or under consideration. These initiatives are seen as a means to address both a post-Afghanistan world and reduced force levels resulting from budgetary constraints.

Special Purpose MAGTFs - Crisis Response (SPMAGTF-CR)[31]

In the wake of the September 11, 2012, attack on the U.S. diplomatic personnel and facilities in Benghazi, Libya, DOD reportedly approved the creation of a new 550 person Marine crisis-response force centered on a reinforced Marine rifle company, six MV-22B Ospreys and two KC-130J Hercules tanker planes. This unit is under the control of the Commander of U.S. Africa Command (USAFRICOM) and has elements based in Moron Airbase in Spain and Sigonella Naval Air Station in Italy. This response force is not reliant on U.S. naval ships and is designed to be able to fly quickly for missions such as embassy reinforcement to humanitarian assistance. In July 2013, during a period of intense tension in Egypt, this unit was reportedly put on alert to help secure the U.S. embassy in Cairo or to help U.S. citizens leave the country, if required.

Reports further suggest that additional SPMAGTF-CRs might be stood up for South America and the Middle East as well. It is not known if these additional SPMAGTF-CRs be smaller than 550 personnel, where they will be stationed or when or if these units will be established. In all cases, these SPMAGTF-CRs are not viewed as replacements for MEUs or other Marine forces but are instead envisioned as assets that a geographic combatant commander can call upon with little or no notice to help respond to a potential crisis or in the aftermath of an attack or humanitarian crisis.

Expansion of Marine Security Guard Program

As a result of September 11, 2012, Benghazi attack, Congress authorized 1,000 additional Marine security guards beginning FY 2014.[32] From a CRS Report:[33]

> A provision in the National Defense Authorization Act for Fiscal Year 2013, P.L. 112-239 [Title IV, Subtitle A, Section 404] directs the Secretary of Defense to grow the Marine Security Guard Program in order to increase the number of detachments at U.S. embassies, consulates, and other diplomatic facilities by up to 1,000 Marines during fiscal years 2014 through 2017, and reassess program's focus on the protection of classified information. The measure also requires the President to separate the Program's budget request from that of the Marine Corps as a whole, and it requires reexamination of the Marine units' rules of engagement.

These additional guards are to be assigned to the Marine Corps Embassy Security Group in Quantico, Virginia and will augment the approximately 1,200 Marine security guards currently assigned to U.S. diplomatic facilities in over 130 countries.[34] In theory, these Marines are to be used to increase the size of the Marine Corps Security Detachments at embassies and consulates in what the State Department deems high threat countries. Given the potential and current levels of unrest in some countries in the USAFRICOM and USCENTCOM regions, it is likely that additional Marines will be sent to U.S. diplomatic facilities in selected countries in Africa and the Middle East. A report suggests that three such posts already identified for enhanced Marine presence include Juba, South Sudan; Casablanca, Morocco; and Freetown, Sierra Leone.[35]

Marine Special Operations Command (MARSOC) Regional Assignments and Potential Return to Sea[36]

The Marine Special Operations Command (MARSOC) is a component command of the U. S. Special Operations Command (USSOCOM) and constitutes the Marine Corps' contribution to U.S. Special Operations Forces (SOF). MARSOC is reportedly realigning the responsibilities of its three operational battalions to better support geographical combatant commanders. As part of this realignment, the 1st Marine Special Operations Battalion (MSOB) from Camp Pendleton, CA will align to the U.S. Pacific Command (USPACOM) region while the 2nd and 3rd MSOBs out of Camp Lejeune, NC will align with USCENTCOM and USAFRICOM respectively. These units are to receive appropriate language and cultural training so they will be better attuned to their areas of operation. In another initiative designed to get special operations forces back at sea with MEUs—a common practice prior to September 11, 2001 when Navy SEALs would deploy with MEUs— MARSOC began training with the 11th MEU to facilitate future deployments with Marine expeditionary forces. A timetable for when MARSOC units will be integrated with deploying MEUs has not yet been made public and the relationship with Marine Force Reconnaissance units (who had assumed special operations missions in the absence of the Navy SEALs) has not yet been established.

SELECTED EXTERNAL PERSPECTIVES: MARINE CORPS ROLES, MISSIONS, AND FORCE STRUCTURE

While there has been a great deal of Marines Corps introspection as to future roles, missions, and how the force should be structured, other institutions are also examining these very same questions. Far from a purely academic exercise, this examination is bounded by the budgetary constraints facing the Marine Corps and its sister services. A sample of some proposals that might merit future discussion include:

The Marines and Special Operations Forces (SOF) Responsible for Worldwide Ground Engagement[37]

This article in Joint Forces Quarterly, published by the National Defense University, proposes that U.S. SOF and Marine MAGTFs should be the lead instruments for land engagement operations with other countries. Engagement activities are viewed as both indirect and preventative in nature and run the gamut from training other nation's military forces, participating in military exercises, and other activities which involve constructive interaction between U.S. and foreign military personnel. In terms of land-oriented engagement operations, the U.S. Army is focusing a significant level of effort in world-wide engagement activities - particularly aspiring to operations in the Asia-Pacific region - in order to "prevent" future conflicts and, if unable to prevent a conflict, at least "shape" its outcome.

The article's authors argue that U.S. SOF and Marine MAGTFs should instead take the lead in DOD engagement activities on land. They contend that SOF and the Marines "both possess capabilities and cultures for early and successful initial ground engagement in the exceedingly complex, unpredictable, and unstructured world that confronts the U.S. military."[38] They envision the Marines and SOF undertaking such engagement activities designed to avoid larger and more costly interventions. The Marines, they suggest, are optimally configured in their expeditionary role to provide rapid response not just to engagement opportunities but to humanitarian crises, traditional power projection operations, and forced entry operations if required.

Restructuring the Operational Force[39]

Distributed and Decentralized Forces

A study conducted by the Center for Strategic and Budgetary Assessments (2008) and an article in the Naval War College Review (2012) propose the Marines improve their ability to operate with smaller and more independent units in a highly distributed geographic manner. These small teams would be designed to be highly mobile and capable of conducting low-signature amphibious landings and could also designate targets for airstrikes as well as naval gunfire and missile strikes. These smaller, distributed units could be ideal in dealing with pirates and small, non-state terrorist organizations and would be well-suited for conducting raids and other short duration operations. In a less lethal role, these units could also conduct train-and-advise operations with friendly military forces operating in a remote field environment. These types of units could also meet the U.S. strategic intent of conducting "light foot print" operations whenever possible.

Focus on Company and Battalion-Sized Forces[40]

Both the Center for Strategic and Budgetary Assessments study and the Naval War College article support and expand on the findings of the Marine's 2010 Force Structure Review Group study[41] which contends the Marines should occupy a "sweet spot" with respect to joint forces, lying between an Army regiment [in actuality this would be an Army Brigade Combat Team (BCT) as the Army does not typically organize for combat as a regiment] and a special operations team (about a platoon-sized organization). This "sweet spot" is further defined as the company to battalion level and the authors suggest the Marines should emphasize company and battalion level operations and should focus their efforts and resources at this lower level of employment. This lower level emphasis could not only address DOD's "light foot print" aspiration but might also be more cost efficient in an era of budgetary constraints. The recent creation of SPMAGTF-CRs built around a reinforced Marine rifle company could prove to be a model for this lower level focus. In terms of Marine forces afloat, the Center for Strategic and Budgetary Assessments[42] suggests the creation of a littoral operations MAGTF consisting of a reinforced Marine rifle company embarked on an LPD-17[43] amphibious transport and two or three Littoral Combat Ships (LCS).[44] The author contends that this particular force mix would be well-suited for the types of operational challenges likely to be faced by the Naval Services in the future.

Marine Aviation[45]

In "Marching Towards the Sweet Spot: Options for the U.S. Marine Corps in a Time of Austerity," the author acknowledges the contentious issue of Marine Aviation, noting that questions as to the need for the Marines to have their own dedicated air arm have been in existence since the post-World War II unification movement and continue to this day. The Marines have argued the justification for having their own tactical air force is the "uniqueness" of the Marine Corps combined arms team and if their air arm was reduced or eliminated, the other services would have to fill the void.

Given DOD's current and anticipated fiscal austerity, one suggestion would be to eliminate "high-end" fixed wing aircraft such as the F-35B short takeoff and vertical landing variant of the Lightning II multi-role fighter[46] and instead rely on Navy aircraft for fixed-wing close air support. Aside from fixed-wing air support, in keeping with the Marines' focus on smaller infantry unit operations, a more affordable mix of tactical air support might be adopted, using rotary-wing, unmanned platforms, and modified cargo aircraft such as the KC-130J Harvest Hawk gunship variant or modified MV-22 Ospreys might be pursued. This new mix might be more in keeping with the types contingency operations that the Marines are more likely to face in the future as opposed to major theater wars which many experts feel are a much more remote possibility.

Move Selected Capabilities into the Reserves[47]

Some analysts believe the Marines are attempting to balance three identities: a forward-deployed amphibious force; the small-wars force of choice; and a force that fights the nation's major land wars. Some believe that twelve years of conflict in Iraq and Afghanistan, where the Marines were tasked to function as a second land army, made the Marines "become too heavy, too removed from their expeditionary, amphibious roots, and the unique skill sets those missions require."[48] If the Marine Corps opts for a more expeditionary, crisis response type of force, many of the capabilities needed for fighting a major land war could be shifted to the reserve component. The Marine Corps Reserves have been touted as a success story during Operation Iraqi Freedom as they did not require an extensive train up period to achieve an acceptable level of operational effectiveness. Some of the major warfighting capabilities viewed as candidates for being moved into the reserves include tank, artillery, and aviation command and control units that support wing-level task forces.[49] In addition, fixed-wing Marine aviation units needed to support major theater operations could also be moved to the Marine

Corps Reserve as operations of this nature have historically permitted time to buildup forces.[50]

POTENTIAL ISSUES FOR CONGRESS

Marine Corps Roles and Missions

Historically, eras of declining or constrained defense budgets have served as "forcing functions" ushering in changes in service's roles and missions and force structure. Perhaps in the current era of sequestration, redundancies between the Marines and the Army are an issue worth examination.

Should the Marines Be Given the Leading Role in the Pacific?

The Administration's 2012 strategic shift to the Pacific region could present an opportunity to both focus resources and eliminate redundancies. The U.S. Naval Institute notes:

> Former Marine Corps deputy commandant for aviation Lt. Gen. George Trautman agreed that the service will return to its traditional role in the vast stretches of the Pacific. "The presence of strength breeds prosperity and peace," he said.
>
> The Marines have been in the Pacific theater continuously over the past 70 years to keep the peace, he said, and that presence will continue to grow as the United States rebalances its forces to the region. Anytime a crisis emerges, the Marines are usually the first to respond, be it a humanitarian disaster or some kind of unanticipated military crisis.
>
> The service plans to keep a force of Marines deployed to Darwin, Australia, as part of the renewed interest the region, for example, Trautman says. Additionally, forces are being redistributed from Okinawa, Japan, to both Guam and Hawaii. Meanwhile, the doors are being reopened to training in Thailand and the Philippines, he added.
>
> "Marines will be used all over the Pacific in small packets," Work said. Those units will respond to any number of different types of contingencies. Moreover, the Marine Corps has strong ties with partners in the region. One example is the island nation of Singapore. "The partnership between Marine Aviation and Singapore air force is as solid as can be," Trautman said. Meanwhile, the service also has historic ties with the South Korea's Marine Corps, which is closely modeled on its American counterpart.[51]

In a similar effort, the U.S. Army is seeking to assert itself in the region, with some analysts suggesting that in a post Iraq and Afghanistan world - where few foresee the U.S. getting involved costly, long term land operations - the Army is in search of a mission and has decided to make engagement in the Asia-Pacific region a priority. Other than a significant presence in South Korea, the Army does not have the history or presence that Marines enjoy in the Pacific.

One recent report suggests Army efforts to reassert itself in the Pacific are being undertaken to develop a strategic narrative and an argument to prevent future Army personnel cuts.[52] While some have asserted the Army is trying to create a second Marine Corps in the Pacific and building a force that the nation doesn't need, the Army claims that it has a long, unbroken history in the Pacific. This situation has evolved into what has been described as a "turf war" in the Pacific, a not uncommon occurrence between the Army and Marines, particularly during post-war periods when forces are reduced and defense budgets decline.

Perhaps, instead of competing for missions in the Pacific where the Marines are currently established, the Marines could be allocated the lead role in the Pacific region and the Army could be assigned the lead in another region better suited to the Army's land-centric focus. Such an allocation might help to avoid redundancy and associated costs and perhaps help the Army reallocate resources that it would use to expand its Pacific presence to other areas such as training and maintenance that are suffering due to decreased funding.

Should the Marines' Focus Be Primarily Crisis Response?

Assigning the leading role of crisis response to the Marines could help to decrease redundancy and also achieve a level of cost savings for both the Army and Marine Corps. As previously noted, in addition to MEUs stationed at sea around the world, the Marines have created a SPMAGTF-CR for the USAFRICOM region and could possibly create additional units to support other geographic combatant commanders. In a similar move, the Chief of Staff of the Army has reportedly directed the creation of company-sized unit quick-response forces for each geographic combatant commander to perform essentially the same tasks as the Marines SPMAGT-CRs.[53] These Army units, formed around a conventional infantry company, would be required to respond within 18 to 24 hours, but such a response could prove to be difficult as the vast majority of the Active Army will be based in the continental United States after 2014. In contrast, in addition to the MEUs afloat, the Marines envision stationing their crisis response units forward in theater where they would likely have a better response time than Army units and would also have the benefit of their own organic CV-22 and KC-130 aircraft to self-deploy their forces.

If the Marines are to focus primarily on crisis response, this could provide them with the opportunity to perhaps "slim down" the force by focusing instead on what types of force structure and equipment would be required for response to natural disasters, enhanced protection of U.S. diplomatic facilities and personnel, and limited raid-like combat operations. A clear delineation of who has the lead responsibility for crisis response might also permit the Army to eliminate some of its crisis response force structure and instead focus its limited budget resources on post-crisis follow-on operations and traditional land combat. For example, the Army reportedly has a requirement for 49,000 paratroopers according to the 2012 Defense Planning Guidance, with one entire division—the 82nd Airborne Division from Ft. Bragg, N.C.—devoted primarily to crisis response.[54] While a need for an Army airborne assault capability exists from a joint perspective, perhaps a large scale, "ready to deploy at a moment's notice" capability might no longer be appropriate given anticipated future security challenges.[55] If the Marines were designated the lead service for crisis response, both services might be presented with an opportunity to better focus their resources and training and thereby increase overall effectiveness. While some defense officials might argue that the Marines and Army must have separate and distinct crisis response capabilities and associated forces, an argument might be made that a degree of specialization could actually be more effective and cost efficient over time.

How Much Amphibious Assault Capability Does the Marine Corps Need?

According to the 2010 report of the Marine Corps Force Structure Review Group, the Marines require the forces, ships, and equipment to accommodate the assault echelons of two MEBs.[56] In April 2012, the Marine Corps published the results of an Amphibious Capabilities Working Group study on naval amphibious capability. The study, *Naval Amphibious Capability in the 21st Century: Strategic Opportunity and a Vision for Change*, states the United States is a maritime nation with critical maritime interests, noting 90% of global commerce that travels by sea is most vulnerable where sea meets land in the littorals.[57] The study further finds "for a maritime nation with global interests, a minimal two brigade amphibious force represents a sound investment in ensuring access for the rest of the joint force."[58]

While U.S. Code, Title 10, Section 5063 sets out the requirements for the Marines and Navy to maintain an amphibious assault capability, there is discretion as to "how much" of this capability is required. If the Marines choose to focus on smaller, battalion and company-level operations based on analysis of likely future threats, then there might be an opportunity to look at this requirement for two MEB's worth of capability which could have an impact on Marine Corps force structure and equipment programs[59] and Navy shipbuilding.

Marine Corps Force Structure

If the Marine Corps draws down to a 174,000 or lower active endstrength, there might be opportunities to modify force structure to reflect both a smaller Marine Corps and the types of future threats that it might face.

Marine Forces Afloat

As previously discussed, the Marines maintain two to three MEUs at sea to respond to crises as well as other military operations as directed. As the Marine Corps adapts to accommodate a smaller active force, a strategic shift to the Pacific, and an emerging security environment where smaller, localized threats to U.S. security interests are more likely than major theater conflicts, a reexamination of the traditional MEU might be in order. Marine leadership may have already taken the first step by creating forward-deployed, land-based SPMAGTF-CRs. To provide a ship-based complement, perhaps littoral operations MAGTF consisting of a reinforced Marine rifle company embarked on a LPD-17 accompanied by a couple of LCSs as previously proposed might be appropriate in some circumstances. While the littoral MAGTF might not be the Marines chosen solution, a smaller MEU construct might permit the Marines and Navy to provide more global coverage than the existing two to three embarked MEUs.

Emphasis on Battalion and Company-Sized Units

In order to fill the "sweet spot" between special forces and an Army BCT, the Marines might choose to make company and battalion-sized units the focus of its force structure initiatives. This force level could prove to be appropriate for the types of crisis response missions the Marines could be asked to respond to as well as any engagement or security assistance operations they might be asked to perform. A potential benefit of this focus could be the elimination or reduction of higher echelon headquarters and support units (possibly regimental-level) which could also greatly facilitate both decentralized and distributed operations. This emphasis also recognizes the claim that military technological innovations over the past decade such as information technology, unmanned systems, and precision weaponry have given smaller units of action significantly more capability than their predecessors.

Should More of the Marines' Major Warfighting Capability be Placed in the Reserves?

If the Marines are determined to return to their expeditionary roots and avoid becoming a de facto "second land army" perhaps one course of action might be to place an increased portion of forces and weapons systems that are more suited for major regional conflicts into the Marine Corps Reserve. Such realignment could permit the Marines to pursue material solutions better suited for crisis response operations. More expensive systems such as tanks, artillery, and high performance aircraft - which would probably be of little use in embassy security or humanitarian support missions - might prove to be better suited for placement in the Marine Corps Reserves. A number of DOD and civilian studies suggest that reserve forces when not deployed are a more affordable alternative than maintaining these forces on active duty, particularly those types of units that do not have a great deal of utility except in certain scenarios, such as armor units. In this regard, such a rebalancing of the Marine Corps active and reserve components might enable the Marine to avoid additional cuts in infantry and aviation units if the decision is made to reduce the Marines active endstrength below 174,000.

End Notes

[1] Endstrength is the number of military personnel needed to accomplish a service's statutory mission. It is also the number of personnel that a service is authorized to have by the end of a fiscal year. For additional information on endstrength see CRS Report R43184, FY2014 National Defense Authorization Act: Selected Military Personnel Issues, coordinated by Don J. Jansen.

[2] U.S. Marine Corps Concepts & Programs 2013, America's Expeditionary Force in Readiness, 2013, p. 11.

[3] U.S. Code, Title 10, Section 5063, United States Marine Corps: Composition and Functions, January 3, 2012, p. 1962.

[4] Marine Corps Operating Concepts, Third Edition, June 2010, p. 9.

[5] U.S. Marine Corps Concepts & Programs 2011, America's Expeditionary Force in Readiness, 2011, p. 54.

[6] James K. Sanborn, "Restructuring of Active Force Likely Means Big Changes for the Reserves," Marine Corps Times, September 30, 2013.

[7] Information is from Marine Corps Operating Concepts, Third Edition, June 2010 and Marine Legislative Liaison Office. Note these numbers include attached Navy personnel: (corpsmen, religious personnel, etc.)

[8] Information in this section is taken from U.S. Marine Corps Concepts & Programs 2013, America's Expeditionary Force in Readiness, 2013, pp. 12-15.

[9] For information on U.S. naval vessels associated with embarked Marine forces see Appendix A of CRS Report RL34476, Navy LPD-17 Amphibious Ship Procurement: Background, Issues, and Options for Congress, by Ronald O'Rourke.

[10] For information on ARGs see, http://www.navy.mil/navydata/nav_legacy.asp?id=148, accessed November 7, 2013.

[11] Raids are small, short duration combat operations against specific targets.

[12] Information from this section is taken from U.S. Department of Defense News Transcript, "DOD News Briefing with Secretary Gates and Admiral Mullen from the Pentagon," January 6, 2011.

[13] Information in this section is taken from "Reshaping America's Expeditionary Force in Readiness," Report of the 2010 Marine Corps Force Structure Review Group, March 14, 2011.

[14] Ibid., pp. 2-3.

[15] For additional information on Marine Special Operations Command see CRS Report RS21048, U.S. Special Operations Forces (SOF): Background and Issues for Congress, by Andrew Feickert.

[16] Information in this section is taken from U.S. Department of Defense News Transcript, "Major Budget Decisions Briefing from the Pentagon," presented by Secretary of Defense Leon E. Panetta and Chairman of the Joint Chiefs of Staff General Martin E. Dempsey, January 26, 2012; U.S. Department of Defense News Transcript, "Major Budget Decisions Briefing from the Pentagon," presented by Deputy Secretary of Defense Ashton B. Carter and Vice Chairman of the Joint Chiefs of Staff Admiral James A. Winnefeld Jr., January 26, 2012; and U.S. Department of Defense Publication, Sustaining U.S. Global Leadership: Priorities for 21st Century Defense, January 2012.

[17] For additional information on the Pacific strategy see CRS Report R42448, Pivot to the Pacific? The Obama Administration's "Rebalancing" Toward Asia, coordinated by Mark E. Manyin.

[18] Information in this section is taken from U.S. Department of Defense, "Statement on Strategic Choices and Management Review," July 31, 2013.

[19] Ibid.

[20] Information in this section is taken from Donna Miles, "Senate Appoints Four Members to the QDR Panel," American Forces Press Service, March 6, 2013.

[21] The National Defense Authorization Act (NDAA) for Fiscal Year 1997 established the requirement for a QDR in 1997. "The Secretary of Defense shall every four years, ...conduct a comprehensive examination (to be known as a "quadrennial defense review") of the national defense strategy, force structure, force modernization plans, infrastructure, budget plan, and other elements of the defense program and policies of the United States with a view toward determining and expressing the defense strategy of the United States and establishing a defense program for the next 20 years. Each such [QDR] shall be conducted in consultation with the Chairman of the Joint Chiefs of Staff." USC 10, §118(a).

http://www.defense.gov/qdr/QDR_101_FACT_SHEET_January_2010.pdf,   accessed
November 12, 2103.

[22] Briefing given by LTG R.T. Tryon, Expeditionary Warfare Conference, U.S. Marine Corps
Forces Command, October 30, 2013.

[23] Statement of General James F. Amos, Commandant of the Marine Corps Before the Senate
Armed Services Committee on Sequestration, November 7, 2013, p. 7.

[24] James K. Sanborn, "A Force of 174,000," Marine Corps Times, September 30, 2013.

[25] For additional information on MARSOC see CRS Report RS21048, U.S. Special Operations
Forces (SOF): Background and Issues for Congress, by Andrew Feickert.

[26] Hope Hodge Seck, "What Stays, What Goes at 174,000 Marines," Marine Corps Times,
November 4, 2013.

[27] Ibid.

[28] James K. Sanborn, "A Force of 174, 000," Marine Corps Times, September 30, 2013.

[29] Ibid.

[30] Information in this section is taken from James K. Sanborn, "Cutting to 174,000—Or Below,"
Marine Corps Times, October 28, 2013.

[31] Information in this section is taken from Dan Lamothe, "3-Star Details New Marine Crisis-
Response Force," Marine Corps Times, April 21, 2013; Dan Lamothe, "Crisis-Response
Force Put on Alert for Egyptian Unrest," Marine Corps Times, July 15, 2013; Gina Harkins,
"U.S. Crisis-Response Force Coming to Central, S. America," Marine Corps Times, August
29, 2013; and Dan Lamothe, "Preparing for Chaos," Marine Corps Times, September 30,
2013.

[32] Gina Harkins, "Expert: USMC Embassy Guard Boost Will be Tough," Marine Corps Times,
December 21, 2012.

[33] CRS Report R42834, Securing U.S. Diplomatic Facilities and Personnel Abroad: Background
and Policy Issues, by Alex Tiersky and Susan B. Epstein, May 7, 2013, p. 20.

[34] Gina Harkins, "Expert: USMC Embassy Guard Boost Will be Tough," Marine Corps Times,
December 21, 2012.

[35] Gina Harkins, "Marine Security Guards Stand Up New Posts in Africa," Marine Corps Times,
June 28, 2013.

[36] Hope Hodge Seck, "MARSOC Battalions Get New Regional Assignments," Marine Corps
Times, September 30, 2013, and Dan Lamothe, "MARSOC Returns to Sea with the 11th
MEU," Marine Corps Times, June 9, 2013.

[37] Information in this section is taken from Kevin D. Stringer and Katie M. Sizemore, "The
Future of U.S. Landpower, Special Operations Versatility, Marines Corps Utility," Joint
Forces Quarterly (JFQ), Issue 69, 2nd Quarter 2013, pp. 84-90.

[38] Ibid., p. 87.

[39] Information in this section is taken from Robert P. Kozloski, "Marching Toward the Sweet
Spot: Options for the U.S. Marine Corps in a Time of Austerity," Naval War College
Review, 2012 and Dakota L. Wood, "The U.S. Marine Corps: Fleet Marine Forces for the
21st Century," Center for Strategic and Budgetary Assessments, Washington D.C., 2008.

[40] Ibid.

[41] See "Reshaping America's Expeditionary Force in Readiness," Report of the 2010 Marine
Corps Force Structure Review Group, March 14, 2011.

[42] Dakota L. Wood, "The U.S. Marine Corps: Fleet Marine Forces for the 21st Century," Center
for Strategic and Budgetary Assessments, Washington D.C., 2008, p. xv.

[43] For additional information on the LPD-17 see CRS Report RL34476, Navy LPD-17 Amphibious Ship Procurement: Background, Issues, and Options for Congress, by Ronald O'Rourke.

[44] For additional information on the LCS see CRS Report RL33741, Navy Littoral Combat Ship (LCS) Program: Background and Issues for Congress, by Ronald O'Rourke.

[45] Information in this section is taken from Robert P. Kozloski, "Marching Toward the Sweet Spot: Options for the U.S. Marine Corps in a Time of Austerity," Naval War College Review, 2012.

[46] For additional information on the F-35 see CRS Report RL30563, F-35 Joint Strike Fighter (JSF) Program, by Jeremiah Gertler.

[47] Information in this section is taken from Robert P. Kozloski, "Marching Toward the Sweet Spot: Options for the U.S. Marine Corps in a Time of Austerity," Naval War College Review, 2012; Dakota L. Wood, "The U.S. Marine Corps: Fleet Marine Forces for the 21st Century," Center for Strategic and Budgetary Assessments, Washington D.C., 2008; and Marc Gunzinger, "Shaping America's Future Military, Center for Strategic and Budgetary Assessments, Washington D.C., 2013.

[48] Gunzinger, p. 47 quoting a Secretary of Defense Robert Gates lecture.

[49] Kozloski, p. 29.

[50] Ibid., p. 31.

[51] Dave Majumdar, "The Future of the Marines Corps, U.S. Naval Institute, June 14, 2013.

[52] Information in this section is taken from Rajiv Chandrasekaran, "Army's Pacific Pathways' Sets up Turf Battle with the Marines," The Washington Post, December 29, 2013.

[53] Michelle Tan, "Army Quick-Response Forces Stood Up Around the World," Army Times, November 11, 2013.

[54] Brett Barrouquere, "Army Drops Number of Paratroops," Army Times, November 30, 2013.

[55] It should be noted that in terms of a short notice, world-wide airborne capability, the Army's 75th Ranger Regiment also has such a capability and, as a special operations force, is extensively trained to conduct a variety of operations in demanding environments.

[56] "Reshaping America's Expeditionary Force in Readiness," Report of the 2010 Marine Corps Force Structure Review Group, March 14, 2011, p. 2.

[57] Information in this section was taken from "Naval Amphibious Capability in the 21st Century: Strategic Opportunity and a Vision for Change," a report of the Amphibious Capabilities Working Group, April 27, 2012.

[58] Ibid., p. 12.

[59] For information on Marine amphibious assault vehicles see CRS Report R42723, Marine Corps Amphibious Combat Vehicle (ACV) and Marine Personnel Carrier (MPC): Background and Issues for Congress, by Andrew Feickert.

In: Force Reduction
Editor: Geoffrey Hopkins

ISBN: 978-1-63117-586-2
© 2014 Nova Science Publishers, Inc.

Chapter 2

ARMY DRAWDOWN AND RESTRUCTURING: BACKGROUND AND ISSUES FOR CONGRESS[*]

Andrew Feickert

SUMMARY

On January 26, 2012, senior DOD leadership unveiled a new defense strategy based on a review of potential future security challenges, current defense strategy, and budgetary constraints. This new strategy envisions a smaller, leaner Army that is agile, flexible, rapidly deployable, and technologically advanced. This strategy will rebalance the Army's global posture and presence, emphasizing where potential problems are likely to arise, such as the Asia-Pacific region and the Middle East.

As part of the Administration's original proposal, two armored brigade combat teams (ABCTs) in Europe were to be eliminated out of a total of eight BCTs that would be cut from Active Army force structure. The Army had originally stated that it might cut more than eight BCTs from the Army's current 44 Active BCTs. Army endstrength would go from 570,000 in 2010 to 490,000 by the end of 2017. As part of this reduction, the Army would no longer be sized to conduct large-scale, protracted stability operations but would continue to be a full-spectrum force capable of addressing a wide range of national security challenges. The Army National Guard and Army Reserves were not targeted for

---

[*] This is an edited, reformatted and augmented version of a Congressional Research Service publication, CRS Report for Congress R42493, from www.crs.gov, prepared for Members and Committees of Congress, dated October 25, 2013.

significant cuts. Army leadership stated the impending decrease in Active Duty Army force structure would place an even greater reliance on the National Guard and Reserves.

On June 25, 2013, the Army announced it would cut 12 BCTs from the Active Army as well as a number of unspecified support and headquarters units. As part of this initiative, infantry and armored BCTs would receive a third maneuver battalion plus additional engineering and fires capabilities. In addition, National Guard BCTs would also be restructured in a similar fashion. Due to the impact of sequestration, the Army also decided to accelerate the Active Army drawdown to 490,000 soldiers by two years—these cuts would now need to be completed by the end of 2015. In an effort to reduce costs, the Army also announced that it would examine cutting all two-star and higher headquarters staffs by 25%—a figure that includes soldiers, Army civilians, and contractors.

There will likely be a human dimension of the Army's drawdown. Troops have received an unprecedented level of support from the American public, and those soldiers leaving the service—voluntarily and perhaps involuntarily—might have strong personal feelings about leaving the Army and their comrades after multiple deployments to combat zones. The Army drawdown will likely be achieved in large degree by controlling accessions (i.e., the number of people allowed to join the Army). If limiting accessions is not enough to achieve the desired endstrength targets, the Army can employ a variety of involuntary and voluntary drawdown tools authorized by Congress, such as Selective Early Retirement Boards (SERBs) and Reduction-inForce (RIF). Voluntary tools that the Army might use include the Voluntary Retirement Incentive, the Voluntary Separation Incentive, Special Separation Bonuses, Temporary Early Retirement Authority, the Voluntary Early Release/Retirement Program, and Early Outs.

The Administration's proposals to drawdown and restructure the Army raise some potential issues for congressional consideration. These questions include the potential impacts of accelerating the Army's drawdown by two years and whether the current Active Component/Reserve Component force mix should be reexamined.

IMPORTANCE TO CONGRESS

The Administration's proposal to reduce the size of the Army as well as restructure units and headquarters has national security implications that Congress will need to consider as part of its oversight and authorizations and appropriations role. In terms of size of the force, Congress sets the endstrength for both the Active and Reserve components of the Army. Congress also authorizes and appropriates funds needed for Army restructuring, training exercises, equipment, basing, and infrastructure, as well as the various manpower management tools the Army could use to drawdown the force. Administration decisions about the structure of the Army can have a significant impact on Army bases in a Member's district or state, which can also have economic ramifications for communities around or near affected bases. The Administration's downsizing and restructuring proposals also can have a significant impact on local and state defense-related industries. Lastly, soldiers and their families who might be affected by the Administration's decisions constitute a unique element of Members' constituencies.

THE ADMINISTRATION'S DECISION TO DRAWDOWN AND RESTRUCTURE THE ARMY

Most experts would agree the Administration's decision to reduce the size of the Army was an outgrowth of its decision to withdraw U.S. forces from Iraq by the end of 2011 and the stated intent of handing over security responsibilities for Afghanistan to the Afghan government and Afghan National Army by the end of 2014. The United States has routinely drawn down forces upon the completion of a major conflict, eschewing a "large standing army" during peacetime— although it can be argued that in a post-9/11 world, "peacetime" is a somewhat subjective term. A brief history of past Army drawdowns can be found at *Appendix B*.

BACKGROUND

The foundation for the Army's drawdown and restructuring was laid in early 2011. A year later in January 2012, the Administration provided additional details on proposed force structure and global posture.

January 6, 2011, News Briefing with Secretary of Defense Gates and Chairman Admiral Mullen[1]

On January 6, 2011, Secretary of Defense Robert Gates and Chairman of the Joint Chiefs of Staff Admiral Mike Mullen held a news briefing "announcing a number of decisions and measures that mark the next major step in this department's reform agenda." These decisions and measures, largely taken in response to fiscal pressures, involved a variety of cross-service actions, including consolidating and eliminating headquarters and organizations, modifying or eliminating weapon systems programs, and force reductions. Army force structure-specific actions included

- reduce Active Army endstrength by 27,000 troops starting in 2015, and
- acknowledgement there was "excess" force structure in Europe but no action would be taken until 2015 or without consultation with allies.

Secretary Gates noted the Army was also in the process of divesting itself of an additional 22,000 troops who were temporarily authorized in 2010 and this temporary endstrength would be eliminated by 2013. Combined with the 27,000 Active permanent endstrength reductions that will start in 2015, this represents a reduction of 49,000 Active Duty troops from FY2011 levels.

January 26, 2012, Administration Major Budget Decision Briefing[2]

On January 26, 2012, senior DOD leaders unveiled a new defense strategy, based on a review of the defense strategy at the time and budgetary constraints. This new strategy envisioned

- a smaller, leaner military that is agile, flexible, rapidly deployable, and technologically advanced;
- rebalancing global posture and presence, emphasizing where potential problems are likely to arise, such as the Asia-Pacific region and the Middle East;
- maintaining presence elsewhere in the world (Europe, Africa, and Latin America), using innovative partnerships, strengthening key alliances, and developing new partnerships;
- being able to quickly confront and defeat aggression from any adversary anytime, anyplace; and

- protecting and prioritizing key investments in technology and new capabilities as well as the capacity to grow, adapt, mobilize, and surge when needed.

During this briefing, the following Army force structure decisions were highlighted:

- *Asia-Pacific/Middle East:* Sustain Army structure in the Pacific;
- *Europe and Global Partners:*
  - Adjust Our Posture in Europe:
  - Eliminate two forward-stationed Army heavy brigades;
  - Maintain NATO Article 5 commitments[3] and ensure interoperability with allied forces by allocating a U.S.-based brigade to NATO Response Force;[4] and
  - Rotate U.S.-based Army units to Europe for training and exercises.
- Forces No Longer Sized for Long-Term Stability Operations:
  - Reduce Active Army endstrength. Army will go from about 570,000 in 2010 to 490,000 in the Future Year Defense Plan (FYDP); and
  - Preserve expertise in security force assistance and counterinsurgency.
- Protecting the Potential for Future Adjustments:
  - Retain a slightly more senior force in the Active Army to allow growth if needed;
  - Preserve Army organizational structure and training force to allow growth if needed; and
  - Retain a Ready and Capable Reserve Component;
    - Reduce Army National Guard endstrength slightly;
    - Sustain increased readiness prior to mobilization; and
    - Maintain key combat-support and combat service-support capabilities.

In addition to force structure and endstrength decisions, the Administration also made the following specific commitments:

- A significant land force presence would be maintained in Korea as well as an operationally responsive peacetime presence in the Middle East;
- In light of repositioning of forces overseas and eliminating force structure, the President would ask Congress to authorize the use of the base realignment and closure (BRAC) process;
- The new strategic guidelines will require the Army to return to full-spectrum training, develop a versatile mix of capabilities, formations, and equipment to succeed on land, including environments where access will be contested; and
- Align a brigade combat team (BCT) with each geographic combatant command.

JANUARY 2012 DRAWDOWN
AND RESTRUCTURING PROPOSALS

Proposal to Reduce Endstrength[5]

On January 27, 2012, Army Chief of Staff General Odierno noted 90,000 soldiers were deployed in support of operations and another 96,000 soldiers forward-stationed overseas in nearly 150 countries. DOD announced the Army would reduce the size of the Active Army starting in 2012 from a post-9/11 peak in 2010 of about 570,000 soldiers to 490,000 soldiers by the end of 2017. DOD planned for only marginal reductions in the Army National Guard and none in the Army Reserve. Army leadership stated endstrength reductions would "follow a drawdown ramp that allows us to take care of soldiers and families while maintaining a ready and capable force."[6]

Army leaders noted the 490,000-strong Army would have the following advantages over the 482,000-strong Army of 2001:

- a combat-seasoned force;
- increased investments in special operations forces and the cyber domain;
- drastically improved command and control capabilities, which significantly enhance mission command;
- modularized brigade combat teams (BCTs);
- increased aviation assets;

- an operational National Guard and Reserve affording increased depth and capacity; and
- lessons learned over 10 years of combat.[7]

Units to Be Eliminated[8]

During the January 27, 2012, briefing, DOD and Army leaders stated they planned to eliminate at least eight Active Duty BCTs from existing force structure. Army leaders also stated two armored BCTs[9] (ABCTs) would be removed from Europe and these two ABCTs would not be re-stationed in the United States but instead eliminated from Army force structure. On February 16, 2012, the Army issued an information paper to Congress[10] that provided additional details. According to the paper:

- The Army's V Corps Headquarters would not return to Europe upon the completion of its deployment to Operation Enduring Freedom in late FY2013. The long-term future and location of the V Corps Headquarters would be addressed as part of the Total Army Analysis (TAA) process in which overall force structure and endstrength issues are evaluated.
- Two ABCTs would be inactivated (the 170th BCT in FY2013 and the 172nd BCT in FY2014).
- Additional Army enabler forces, potentially in the range of 2,500 soldiers, could be reduced from Europe as part of the TAA process.[11]

Press reports at the time suggested the Army might cut more than eight BCTs Army-wide.[12] These additional cuts would most likely result from a reorganization of the BCT's structure. It was also reported that the Army would cut more ABCTs, as DOD had issued strategic guidance calling for a leaner and more rapidly deployable force. As already noted, the 170th ABCT stationed in Baumholder, Germany, and the 172nd ABCT stationed in Grafenwoehr, Germany, would be eliminated. The 170th ABCT was deactivated on October 9, 2012.[13] In terms of cuts to forces in the Pacific, the Chief of Staff of the Army, General Raymond T. Odierno, reportedly stated Army forces in the Pacific would remain at current levels, with plans to keep Stryker, infantry, and aviation units—about 10,300 soldiers—at Schofield Barracks in Hawaii.[14]

Units to Be Realigned and Restructured[15]

In terms of realigning and restructuring the Active Army, DOD and the Army announced in January 2012 that

- active forces would no longer be sized to conduct large and protracted stability operations;
- Army force structure would be sustained in the Pacific, and a persistent presence would be maintained in the Middle East;
- Army forces will rotate through Europe and other regions on a more frequent basis;
- a U.S.-based heavy brigade would be allocated to the NATO Response Force;
- a brigade combat team (BCT) would be aligned with each geographic combatant command to provide cultural and language training to support engagement operations; and
- BCTs and enabling units would be examined for optimum design, which could lead to further BCT reductions if the Army decides to increase the capability of BCTs.

Press reports offered additional details on how BCTS might be restructured.[16] Prior to the 2003 decision to restructure the Army to a modular force, all combat brigades had three maneuver battalions (infantry, armor, or mechanized infantry). Under modularity, only Stryker battalions have three maneuver battalions, and infantry BCTs (IBCTs) and armored BCTs (ABCTs) have only two, based on a contested belief at the time that additional intelligence, surveillance, and reconnaissance (ISR) units added to the BCT could substitute for the third maneuver battalion. Reportedly, Army leaders who had returned from Iraq and Afghanistan lobbied to add back the third maneuver battalion to IBCTs and ABCTs, arguing this additional battalion could enable more successful combat, patrol, and site-security operations.

Changes in Unit Basing[17]

On January 27, 2012, Secretary of Defense Panetta indicated that he would ask Congress to authorize a Base Realignment and Closure (BRAC) process whereby bases in the United States can be realigned or closed. If

Congress approves BRAC, it is likely some Army bases could be realigned or closed, which could require some Army units to move to other new or existing bases. With the reliance on an increased use of rotational forces under the Administration's new strategic guidelines, it is likely a number of smaller bases—some permanent but many temporary—might need to be established to accommodate these rotational forces. In terms of the two ABCTs eliminated from Europe, it is not known what will happen to the Army bases at Baumholder and Grafenwohr.

Impact on the National Guard and Reserve[18]

As previously noted, under DOD's 2012 strategic guidance, the Army intends to

- retain a ready and capable reserve component;
- reduce National Guard endstrength slightly;
- sustain increased readiness prior to mobilization; and
- maintain key combat-support and combat service-support capabilities.

Like previous pronouncements, no specifics were provided regarding reductions in Reserve Component endstrength and how readiness and support capabilities would be maintained.

Chief of Staff of the Army General Raymond T. Odierno reportedly stated the Pentagon's decision to cut the active force by 80,000 soldiers would place greater reliance on the National Guard and Reserves, "particularly if the United States gets into two major long-term combat operations at the same time."[19] The report further noted the United States would be required to keep its reserve forces at a higher state of readiness than it did before the wars in Iraq and Afghanistan. General Odierno suggested if the Army had to fight two large, simultaneous, longterm wars; the United States would rely more heavily on allies and request a large-scale mobilization of the reserves. The reserves would also be used to "buy time to increase the size of the active component," and because of the requirement for higher readiness, a new readiness model would need to be developed to keep the National Guard and Reserves at a higher state of readiness.[20]

RECENT FORCE STRUCTURE ANNOUNCEMENTS

DOD Announces U.S. Army in Europe Force Structure Changes

On March 1, 2013, DOD announced a series of force structure changes for the U.S. Army in Europe from the period 2013 through 2016. The text of the news release is as follows:[21]

DOD Announces U.S. Army in Europe Force Structure Changes

The Department of Defense announced today that Germany-based elements of the 173rd Airborne Brigade Combat Team will relocate within Germany and to Italy in summer 2013. A total of four battalions will be relocated. Two battalions will relocate from Germany to Italy; the brigade's headquarters and one infantry battalion will relocate from Caserma Ederle in Vicenza, Italy, to the Army's new facility in Del Din (formerly known as Dal Molin) in Vicenza. The other two battalions will relocate from Schweinfurt and Bamberg, Germany, to Grafenwoehr, Germany. In addition to the previously announced inactivation of

V Corps Headquarters and the 170th and 172nd Infantry Brigades, the disposition of 2,500 enabling forces are provided as follows:

In 2012:

170th Infantry Brigade, Smith Barracks, Baumholder, Germany – Inactivated 167th Medical Detachment (Optometry), Grafenwoehr, Germany – Inactivated

In 2013:

535th Engineer Company, Warner Barracks, Bamberg, Germany – Inactivates 12th Chemical Company, Conn Barracks, Schweinfurt, Germany – Inactivates V Corps Headquarters, Clay Kaserne, Wiesbaden, Germany – Inactivates 172nd Infantry Brigade, Grafenwoehr, Germany – Inactivates

Headquarters and Headquarters Company, 391st Combat Service Support Battalion, Warner Barracks, Bamberg, Germany – Inactivates

B Detachment, 106th Finance Company, Katterbach Kaserne, Ansbach, Germany – Inactivates

42nd Engineer Company, Warner Barracks, Bamberg, Germany – Returns to the United States

99th Movement Control Team, Aviano Air Base, Italy – Returns to the United States

In 2014:

Headquarters, 18th Engineer Brigade, Conn Barracks, Schweinfurt, Germany – Inactivates

243 Engineer Detachment, Conn Barracks, Schweinfurt, Germany – Inactivates

54th Engineer Battalion, Warner Barracks, Bamberg, Germany – Inactivates

370th Engineer Company, Warner Barracks, Bamberg, Germany – Inactivates

7th Signal Brigade, Ledward Barracks, Schweinfurt, Germany – Inactivates

72nd Signal Battalion, Ledward Barracks, Schweinfurt, Germany – Inactivates

Headquarters and Headquarters Detachment, 95th Military Police Battalion, Sembach Kaserne, Kaiserslautern – Inactivates

630th Military Police Company, Warner Barracks, Bamberg, Germany – Inactivates 464th Military Police Platoon, Camp Ederle, Italy – Inactivates 511th Military Police Platoon, Livorno, Italy – Inactivates

541st Engineer Company, Warner Barracks, Bamberg, Germany – Returns to the United States

In 2015:

230th Military Police Company, Sembach Barracks, Kaiserslautern, Germany – Inactivates

3rd Battalion, 58th Aviation Regiment (Airfield Operations Battalion), Storck Barracks, Illesheim, Germany – Returns to the United States

In 2016:

69th Signal Battalion, Grafenwoehr, Germany – Inactivates

525th Military Police Detachment (Military Working Dogs), Baumholder, Germany - Returns to the United States

1st Battalion, 214th General Support Aviation Regiment structure is reduced at Clay Kaserne, Wiesbaden, by 190 soldier spaces and at Landstuhl Heliport by 50 soldier spaces. Information on the disposition of other units in the closing U.S. military communities of Bamberg and Schweinfurt will be provided in the near future, as those force structure actions are determined. These actions are part of DOD's ongoing restructure of resources worldwide in line with our national defense strategy and in support of combatant commanders, NATO and our European allies.

June 2013 Army Force Structure and Stationing Announcement[22]

On June 25, 2013, the Army announced Active Component force structure decisions and stationing plans that it attributed to the fiscal constraints resulting from of the Budget Control Act of 2011 and the previously cited 2012 Defense Planning Guidance. The Army noted that additional force reductions would be required if "sequestration-driven funding reductions remain unmitigated."[23] In terms of force structure changes the Army stated it would

- Reorganize Infantry and Armored BCTs to restore the third maneuver battalion and increase engineer and fires capability;
- Reduce Active Component BCTs from 45 to 33; and
- Continue to grow aviation, special operations, missile defense, and cyber capabilities.

Specific BCTs to Be Cut Between FY2013 and FY2017

In addition to the previously announced cuts of the 170th and 172nd BCTs in Germany, the Army stated the following 10 BCTs would also be eliminated:

- 4th Stryker BCT, 2nd Infantry Division, Joint Base Lewis-McCord, WA;
- 3rd Armored BCT, 4th Infantry Division, Ft. Carson, CO;
- 3rd Armored BCT, 1st Armored Division, Ft. Bliss, TX;
- 4th Infantry BCT, 1st Infantry Division, Ft. Riley, KS;
- 4th Armored BCT, 1st Cavalry Division, Ft. Hood, TX;
- 4th Infantry BCT, 101st Airborne Division, Ft. Campbell, KY;
- 3rd Infantry BCT, 1st Infantry Division, Ft. Knox, KY;
- 3rd Infantry BCT, 10th Mountain Division, Ft. Drum, NY;
- 2nd Armored BCT, 3rd Infantry Division, Ft. Stewart, GA; and
- 4th Infantry BCT, 82nd Airborne Division, Ft. Bragg, NC.

These reductions will leave the Army with 12 Armored BCTs, 14 Infantry BCTs and seven Stryker BCTs.

As part of this announcement, the Army also noted that it would reduce and reorganize numerous non-BCT units—often referred to as enablers—as part of the drawdown. The Army did not provide specifics on these units as it did the BCTs to be cut, and providing a similar level of detail for these non-BCT units to be eliminated would be particularly helpful to Congress as it examines the potential national security impact of these force reductions.

Army to Accelerate Downsizing[24]

Reports suggest that:

> The impact of sequestration [in fiscal 2013], coupled with the threat of continued sequestration levels of funding, is forcing the Army to implement significant reductions to end-strength, readiness and modernization in order to generate short-term cost savings, we are accelerating the downsizing of the Army's active component end-strength to 490K by FY15 instead of FY17. Additionally, we will maintain a certain number and mix of units at a higher level of readiness to meet contingency requirements.[25]

The implications of shortening the drawdown by two years could be quite profound. A significant level of effort will be involved in the planning and execution of these complex operations. This might also lead to a great deal of turbulence for the soldiers and their families as these units are rapidly disbanded.

How the Army Plans to Achieve Accelerated Downsizing[26]

In order to achieve this accelerated drawdown, the Army reportedly plans to use a "full menu of involuntary separation programs."[27] This new accelerated plan means the Army will reduce the Active Component by almost 42,000 soldiers by the end of September 2015 and that many soldiers with good service records and who are qualified for continued service will be involuntarily separated from the Army. The Army estimates that 5,000 officers and 20,000 enlisted soldiers will be forced to leave active duty through involuntary separation or early retirement. Reportedly, for the first time since the 1970s, the Army plans to convene reduction-inforce, or RIF, boards in early 2014 for captains and majors in over strength year groups. In addition to involuntary separations, the Army will reduce the number of soldiers and officers (usually newly commissioned second lieutenants) it brings into the Army each year.

National Guard to Also Reorganize BCTs[28]

An *Army Times* article also details the Army National Guard's reorganization plans:

> Six of the Guard's 28 BCTs will be reorganized this fiscal year, with the others to follow through fiscal 2018, said Lt. Gen. William Ingram, director of the Army National Guard.
>
> The goal is to have the Guard's primary fighting formations match those in the active Army, Ingram has said.
>
> Under the reorganization, each armored and infantry BCT will receive a third maneuver battalion. The Stryker brigades each have three maneuver battalions.
>
> The BCTs will receive additional engineer and fires capabilities.
>
> Once the reorganization is completed, each BCT will have about 4,500 soldiers, nearly 1,000 more than they do in their current configuration.
>
> The Guard's BCT reorganization will mirror that of the active Army, Ingram said. The plan is to take existing Guard units and align them with the BCTs, he said.
>
> The six BCTs that will be reorganized this fiscal year [FY 2014] are:
>
> - 56th BCT, 36th Infantry Division, Texas National Guard;
> - 29th BCT, Hawaii National Guard;
> - 76th BCT, Indiana National Guard;
> - 79th BCT, California National Guard;
> - 55th BCT, 28th Infantry Division, Pennsylvania National Guard; and
> - 1st BCT, 34th Infantry Division, Minnesota National Guard
>
> Plans call for six more BCTs to be reorganized in fiscal 2015, officials said. Another six will be converted in 2016, and five each will be done in fiscal 2017 and 2018.[29]

Army to Cut Headquarters Staffs[30]

In an effort to decrease costs, Army leadership is reportedly examining the possibility of cutting up to 25% of personnel assigned to two-star and above headquarters. These potential cuts include such organizations as Army Forces Command and Training and Doctrine Command, as well as Army corps and division headquarters. Also eligible for cuts are the Army's service component commands such as Army Africa and Army Pacific, which are part of the United States' nine combatant commands. These personnel cuts are not just limited to soldiers but also to Army civilians and contractors and would occur over the course of five years.

Potential Future Force Structure Cuts[31]

Army leadership as well as a number of defense analysts have warned that if sequestration continues, the Army would likely have to downsize further than the 490,000 active duty force target. Under one scenario, Army leaders note if they are compelled to drawdown to a 420,000 active duty force, the Army would be forced to cut the Army National Guard from 358,000 to 315,000 troops and the Army Reserve from 205,000 to 185,000 soldiers. These cuts would likely result in further BCT, support unit, and headquarters cuts, which would not only have operational implications for the Army— Army leaders have stated that at this force level, it would be a substantial risk to conduct even one sustained major combat operation—but might also further exacerbate personnel turbulence within the force.

FORCE REDUCTION AND FORCE-SHAPING PROGRAMS

Historically, military drawdowns have been rather blunt instruments of national policy. As noted in the earlier descriptions of the drawdowns at the conclusion of World War II and Vietnam, the focus was primarily on immediate reductions in accessions and separating/discharging others as soon as possible. The rapid and poorly planned demobilization of Army forces in the past had a deleterious impact on morale, terminated many aspiring military careers, and released significant numbers of military personnel with limited transition assistance.

The recent post-Cold War drawdown was substantially different. Congress still determined the endstrength levels but provided a number of voluntary and involuntary tools to shape each year group of the force—officer, warrant officer, and enlisted. Voluntary separations were emphasized, and some of the tools had robust financial incentives. Few skills were exempt from consideration, and every soldier was vulnerable for separation at some point during nearly a decade of drawdown. It was also the first time that resources were focused on transition assistance and stressed the importance of working with military alumni, even after their separation. Title 10 Drawdown Authorities are discussed in greater detail in *Appendix A.*

The Human Dimension of a Force Drawdown

For the past decade, U.S. military forces have been engaged in combat operations on two fronts— Iraq and Afghanistan. The deployments to these austere environments have been long—typically 7 to 12 months for ground forces, sometimes involuntarily extended to support surge operations and requiring the use of "Stop Loss" policies.[32] Deployments have also been frequent, sometimes with less than a year between rotations resulting in reduced "dwell time" for both active and reserve component personnel. These conflicts have often been very stressful for servicemembers, spouses, and families as indicated by higher than normal divorce and suicide rates.[33]

Throughout this period, support from the American public and political leaders has been consistent. Many now refer to our servicemembers as "America's Heroes" and honor the wounded as "Wounded Warriors." They return home to welcome ceremonies and spontaneous outbreaks of applause in airports, and even those who may disagree with the war effort have been generally supportive of military personnel. Soon the services will begin to transition from high-tempo combat operations to a more stable training and garrison environment, while simultaneously downsizing and reshaping the force. Those with multiple combat tours may feel that they have lost a common cause. Those with pride in the units that they fought with may now see those units eliminated or friends separated from the service either voluntarily or involuntarily. Those who have experienced a military focused on fighting insurgency on multiple fronts over the past decade will see a shift of emphasis to training for full-spectrum operations and individual professional development. The collective effect of these changes could result in a temporary degradation of individual morale and unit effectiveness. The key for leaders at all levels will be to refocus and minimize these potentially negative impacts. However, reducing accessions has its own implications.

Accessions

It is assumed that the post-Operation Iraqi Freedom (OIF)/Operation Enduring Freedom (OEF) drawdown will focus primarily on reduced accessions, because a reduction in accessions significantly reduces the need for other voluntary and involuntary force shaping actions and their inherent negative implications.

The military acquires or procures new personnel annually—enlisted, warrant officer, and officer—through the enlisted recruiting process and officer accession programs. The number to be recruited or accessed is based on the congressionally established endstrength, which is published annually in the National Defense Authorization Act (NDAA). With a known endstrength, the services can then project losses for the coming year, compare this to the endstrength target, and determine the number to be recruited and trained.

During the years of OIF/OEF, the Army generally recruited approximately 75,000 to 80,000 enlisted soldiers a year, initially to sustain an endstrength of 482,000 and, later, to incrementally grow the force to its eventual target strength of 562,000. As announced in the FY2013 President's Budget,[34] the Army will be required to draw down to an endstrength of 490,000 by FY2017, a reduction of 72,000.[35] With five years to accomplish, it appears that the accessions program could absorb a reduction of nearly 15,000 per year and still sustain the force over time, ensure the right mix of training and experience, and allow for reasonable promotion expectations.

Officer Accessions

In 2008, Congress authorized an increased enrollment at the U.S. Military Academy,[36] from 4,000 to 4,400, and the Army greatly expanded its Officer Candidate School (OCS) program at Fort Benning, GA, while also increasing the size of the Reserve Officer Training Corps (ROTC) program. West Point and ROTC have four-year timelines associated with their programs, but the duration of the OCS program is measured in weeks rather than years. Therefore, to reduce officer accessions, OCS can be quickly ramped down with any additional decrements coming from the ROTC program and potentially reverting the service academies to their previous cap of 4,000 students.

2013 Officer Selective Early Retirement Board (SERB) Announced[37]

On March 22, 2013, the Army announced it would convene a Selective Early Retirement Board (SERB) in August 2013 to involuntarily retire up to 30% of Active Duty Colonels and Lieutenant Colonels. The Army states high retention rates and a reduction in officer requirements among senior officers have resulted in an excess of Colonels and Lieutenant Colonels, thereby necessitating the SERB. In terms of levels of command, Colonels command brigade-sized units and Lieutenant Colonels command battalion-sized units. Both Colonels and Lieutenant Colonels also can serve as staff officers in division and higher level formations.

The SERB will consider Lieutenant Colonels who were not selected for promotion to Colonel two or more times as of the FY2012 Colonel Army Promotion Selection Board and Colonels with a date of rank of August 1, 2008, or earlier (five or more years of active duty time in grade). The SERB will also consider the records of every eligible officer and make recommendations for early retirement based on the best interest of the Army.

Protecting the Institutional Army[38]

In order to quickly reactivate mid-grade leaders in the event of a future ground war—the "retain a slightly more senior force in the Active Army to allow growth if needed" proposal from the January 2012 Drawdown and Restructuring Proposal—the Army plans to insulate from the drawdown about 90,000 soldiers from its institutional, non-operational portion of the service. Army service leaders reportedly will instead take an end strength cut of almost 80,000 soldiers from the operational Army. In order to retain mid-grade leaders needed to reactivate units, the Army had planned to put these personnel in units designed to mentor foreign security forces, but the Army is currently considering putting these individuals in Army educational institutions. If this does become policy, these mid-grade soldiers could replace Department of the Army Civilians and contractors presently serving in many of these billets.

POTENTIAL ISSUES FOR CONGRESS

Impact of Accelerated Drawdown

The Army's decision to accelerate its drawdown from 2017 to 2015 could raise issues for congressional consideration. Some potential issues include the following:

- Will this accelerated drawdown have an adverse impact on readiness and add additional risk?
- Will other units have to modify their deployment schedule to account for units deactivating sooner than originally planned for?
- How will the accelerated drawdown impact new Army procurement programs as well as plans to recapitalize equipment?
- Will this quicker than planned for drawdown have either a detrimental or a positive impact on individual soldier training and education as well as unit training?
- How will soldiers and families be impacted by the accelerated drawdown?
- Could this result in morale problems as affected soldiers are now being asked to leave the service two years earlier than they might have originally planned for?
- How will civilian communities near affected Army bases be impacted by a more rapid drawdown?

Active Component/Reserve Component Force Mix

Many defense experts, anticipating continued budgetary constraints, believe that the Army will have to cut additional endstrength beyond the 490,000 active component cuts already underway. As previously noted:

> Under one scenario, Army leaders note if they are compelled to drawdown to a 420,000 active duty force, the Army would be forced to cut the Army National Guard from 358,000 to 315,000 troops and the Army Reserve from 205,000 to 185,000. These cuts would likely result in further BCT, support unit, and headquarters cuts which would not only have operational implications for the Army - Army leaders have stated that at this force level, it would be a substantial risk to conduct even one sustained major combat operation – but might also further exacerbate personnel turbulence within the force.

If this is indeed the case—that further reductions could result in "a substantial risk to conduct even one sustained major combat operation"—maybe the answer is not to decrease the size of the total Army to potentially dangerous levels but instead to re-visit the Active Component (AC)/Reserve Component (RC) force mix. Advocates for a larger reserve component argue that in many cases, the RC is cheaper than the AC, in part because AC troops receive a more generous pension benefit and make costly change-of-station moves every few years.[39] Pentagon leadership noted that because RC units maintain a lesser degree of readiness, that relying on them too much could put the nation at risk during a crisis.[40] What some are suggesting is that the balance between the AC and RC be reexamined and that potentially some AC units that the Army deems mission-essential be moved into the RC in order to achieve a degree of cost efficiency. This would not be an unprecedented action, as the Army as frequently rebalanced the AC/RC mix, but because this impacts the Active "full-time" Army and the "part-time" National Guard and Army Reserves—both of which have strong constituencies both inside and outside the Army—this tends to be a somewhat sensitive and sometimes contentious undertaking.

Reports suggest that the Pentagon and other institutions are examining the proper balance between the AC and RC as a means of reducing costs and being able to retain a certain level of force structure. Because Congress annually sets both the Active and Reserve endstrengths for the Army, any discussions on rebalancing the AC/RC mix will likely require a great deal of congressional involvement.

APPENDIX A. TITLE 10 DRAWDOWN AUTHORITIES[41]

Several authorities in Title 10 result in involuntary separation. They were used sparingly during the post-Cold War drawdown and always preceded by the offer of voluntary incentives. These involuntary tools include the following:

Title 10 Drawdown Authorities—Involuntary Selective Early Retirement Boards (SERB)[42]

Selective Early Retirement is the involuntary retirement of senior officers who are (1) serving lieutenant colonels or commanders (Navy) who have been twice non-selected for promotion to colonel or captain (Navy) or (2) are serving colonels or captains (Navy) who have at least four years in grade and have not been selected for promotion. If not selected for SERB, an officer cannot be considered for another five years. Those selected must be retired not later than the first day of the seventh month after the Secretary concerned approves the recommendation for retirement. While considered involuntary, those selected will receive retired pay and remain eligible for military healthcare and the other benefits associated with military retirement.

Reduction-in-Force (RIF)[43]

Reduction-in-Force is the second involuntary program available for downsizing the officer cohorts. While SERB is focused on those with 20 or more years of service, RIF is directed at those with more than 6 but less than 20 years of service. While the post-Cold War drawdown emphasized voluntary separations and retirements, RIF was available (but used sparingly) if the voluntary programs did not generate adequate volunteers.

2012 Enlisted Qualitative Service Program (QSP)[44]

On March 14, 2012, the Army announced the initiation of the Enlisted Qualitative Service Program (QSP) directed toward the grades of staff sergeant through command sergeant major. Under these provisions, those soldiers under consideration for this program can opt to separate voluntarily in lieu of being subjected for review by the QSP board.

Title 10 Drawdown Authorities—Voluntary[45]

The drawdown tools available during the post-Cold War drawdown are still available to force planners, with several of them recently reinstated by the FY2012 NDAA. These programs were used extensively during the post-Cold War drawdown of the 1990s. While these tools are available to all of the services, the following descriptions will focus on Army programs for the drawdown. They include the following:

Voluntary Retirement Incentive[46]

The Voluntary Retirement Incentive is the one incentive that was not available during the post-Cold War drawdown; it was introduced in the FY2012 NDAA. This program targets retirement-eligible servicemembers with between 20 and 29 years of service. The amount of the incentive is determined by the Service Secretary but may not exceed the member's annual basic pay. In exchange for the payment, the servicemember agrees to retire. The program is capped at no more than 675 officers, and the program expires on December 31, 2018.

Voluntary Separation Incentive (VSI)[47]

The Voluntary Separation Incentive (VSI) is an incentive that is paid annually for twice the number of years the individual served on active duty. Servicemembers must have served between 6 and 20 years and additional eligibility criteria are established by the Service Secretary. The formula for determining the annual annuity is 2.5% times monthly basic pay at the time of separation, times 12, times the number of years of service. The original authority for this incentive was the National Defense Authorization Act for 1992/1993,[48] which terminated the program on December 31, 2001. The VSI program was reinstated by the FY2012 NDAA[49] for the period December 31, 2011, through December 31, 2018.

Special Separation Bonus (SSB)[50]

The Special Separation Bonus (SSB) is a voluntary separation incentive available to any eligible member of the Armed Forces. SSB is a lump sum payment equal to 15% times years of service (YOS) and 12 times monthly basic pay. To be eligible, members must have served for more than 6 years but for less than 20. Other requirements may be established by the Service Secretary. The original authority for the SSB program also expired on December 31, 2001, but was reinstated by the FY2012 NDAA[51] for the period December 31, 2011, through December 31, 2018.

VSI and SSB were complementary programs that were both offered to eligible populations. The primary difference was that VSI was an annuity program, while SSB represents a lump sum payment. Those who volunteer for VSI or SSB do not receive retirement benefits such as a lifelong annuity and retiree health care benefits, although they may later qualify for retirement through reserve service.

Temporary Early Retirement Authority (TERA)[52]

The Temporary Early Retirement Authority (TERA) provided an opportunity for eligible officers, warrant officers, and enlisted personnel to retire prior to completion of 20 years of service. Those in selected grades and skills could voluntarily retire with as few as 15 years of service. TERA retirees have their retired pay reduced for every year less than 20. However, as a retiree, they remain eligible for retired pay; military healthcare; commissary and exchange privileges; and Morale, Welfare and Recreation activities. The original TERA program expired on September 1, 2002, but has been reauthorized by the FY2012 NDAA. The current program began on December 31, 2011, and extends through December 31, 2018.

Voluntary Early Release/Retirement Program (VEERP)[53]

This voluntary program targeted the most junior and the most senior ends of the officer spectrum, with the incentive being a reduction in service obligation. Junior officers (lieutenants and captains) were permitted to resign prior to fulfilling their active duty obligation (five years for U.S. Military Academy graduates, four years for most ROTC scholarship graduates, and three years for Officer Candidate School graduates). Senior officers (lieutenant colonels and colonels) were permitted to retire at their present rank, waiving one year of the existing retirement eligibility criteria (normally three years). For example, a colonel could retire as a colonel but with only two years in grade, rather than the usual three years. This authority was originally included in the FY1991 NDAA.

"Early Outs"[54]

Service Secretaries have the authority to discharge enlisted servicemembers up to three months prior to the end of their term of enlistment. The FY2012 NDAA[55] expanded the three-month standard to one year with no loss of benefits for the members taking advantage of this opportunity. However, members are not entitled to pay and allowances for the period not served. There is no termination date associated with this authority.

Other Personnel Tools with Drawdown Implications

Enlisted Retention Control Points

The military expects that individual performance will result in the periodic promotion of enlisted personnel as their military experience increases and as their individual responsibility within the organization grows. Those who do not progress in a timely manner may be separated prior to the end of their term of service. This policy is implemented through a series of retention control points that dictate how long a servicemember may remain at the current rank/grade before being promoted. Those who fail promotion in a timely manner can be separated prior to their normal term of service. These retention control points can be adjusted over time and can aid in force shaping by separating those with less potential.

The current and previous Army retention control points are shown in *Table A-1.*

Table A-1. Army Retention Control Points (RCP)
("Shaping the enlisted force through tenure")

Rank	Previous RCP	Current RCP (as of June 1, 2011)
Private and Private First Class	8 years	5 years
Specialist	10 years	8 years
Promotable Specialist	15 years	12 years
Sergeants	15 years	13 years
Promotable Sergeants	20 years	15 years
Staff Sergeants	23 years	20 years

Notes: The previous RCP allowed a Sergeant (E-5) to remain on active duty until retirement eligibility at 20 years of service. With the recent tightening of these standards, a Sergeant must separate at 13 years and only the Staff Sergeant (E-6) may remain until 20 years.

Officer Promotion Non-selection

The military's officer management system is an "up or out" system—officers who fail to promote after being twice considered for the next higher grade may be involuntarily separated. To support the officer manpower requirements during the decade of OIF and OEF, many non-selected officers were selectively continued in their current grade. In addition, the OIF/OEF period was one of unusually high promotion selection rates (opportunity) and reduced time-in-grade (timing) before promotion consideration. With the withdrawal of U.S. forces from Iraq and the gradual drawdown of forces in

Afghanistan, the services are again enforcing the standards for promotion and retention. The promotion timing and opportunity standards established by DOD are shown in *Table A-2.*

Table A-2. Promotion Timing and Opportunity

To Grade	Opportunity	Timing
Major/Lieutenant Commander	80%	10 years +/- 1 year
Lieutenant Colonel/Commander	70%	16 years +/- 1 year
Colonel/Captain	50%	22 year +/- 1 year

Source: DOD Instruction 1320.13, July 22, 2009.

Notes: Major, Lieutenant Colonel, and Colonel apply to the Army, Marine Corps, and Air Force. Lieutenant Commander, Commander, and Captain apply to the Navy.

Most recently, the Air Force involuntarily separated 157 majors who had been twice non-selected for promotion to lieutenant colonel.[56] These officers received separation pay and other transition benefits and may be eligible to transfer to the Air National Guard or Air Force Reserve but their Active Duty careers have ended.

APPENDIX B. BRIEF HISTORY OF PAST ARMY DRAWDOWNS

Post-World War II

During World War II, the Army determined what its reasonable post-war strength should be and developed plans for a peaceful demobilization. Initially, the Army established a post-war goal of an Active and Reserve structure capable of mobilizing 4 million troops within a year of the outbreak of a future war. Later, the Army set the strength of the active ground and air forces at 1.5 million (the Army Air Corps did not become the U.S. Air Force until July 26, 1947, with the enactment of the National Security Act of 1947, P.L. 80-235). The vast majority of servicemembers in the Army during World War II were draftees. The Army's demobilization plans provided for the release of troops on an individual basis based on points. Soldiers received point credits for length of service, combat participation and awards, time spent overseas, and parenthood. Also factoring into the Army's plans was the availability of shipping to bring overseas troops to the United States, as well as the capacity to process the discharged soldiers.

However, pressure for faster demobilization from the public, Congress, and the troops themselves affected the Army's plan for an orderly process. The Army responded by easing eligibility requirements and released half of its 8 million troops by the end of 1945. In early 1946, the Army slowed its return of troops from overseas to meet its constabulatory requirements in Germany and Japan, which elicited another public outcry to speed up demobilization. Public opposition diminished after the Army more than halved its remaining strength during the first six months of 1946.

President Truman was determined to balance the national budget, which also affected the Army's manpower. The Administration's dollar ceiling for FY1947 led to a new maximum Army strength of just over 1 million. In order to reach this new level, the Army stopped draft calls and released all post-war draftees along with any other troops eligible for demobilization. By June of 1947, the Army consisted of 684,000 ground troops and 306,000 airmen. Although considered large for a peacetime Army by American standards, the loss of many capable maintenance specialists resulted in widespread deterioration of equipment. Active Army units were understrength, had many barely trained replacements, and were considered "shadows of the efficient organizations they had been at the end of the war."

This post-war reduction saw the Army go from 8 million soldiers and 89 divisions in 1945 to 591,000 men and 10 divisions by 1950—a 93% reduction in manpower over five years. Half of the Army's 10 divisions were deployed overseas, with Far Eastern Command controlling four infantry divisions on occupation duty in Japan and the European Command controlling one infantry division in Germany. The remaining five divisions (two airborne, two infantry, and one armored division) were stationed in the United States and constituted a general reserve to meet emergencies. All 10 divisions had undergone organizational changes, largely based on wartime experience. Despite this reorganization, 9 out of 10 divisions were well below their authorized strength, with most infantry regiments having only two of their three authorized battalions, for example. Also, most units lacked their organic armored units and lacked their wartime complement of weapons. Whatever weapons and equipment these units had were described as "worn-out leftovers from World War II." The low personnel and equipment readiness levels in 1950 became apparent during the initially weak U.S. military response when the Korean War broke out in June of that year.

Post-Vietnam

During the 1960s, DOD had shaped and sized the Armed Forces to fight two and a half wars simultaneously. The wars were two major theater wars, or MTWs—a war in Europe and one in Asia—and a "half war," a small-scale contingency operation. The force to fight this two-and-ahalf-war construct numbered over 950,000 through the middle of the 1960s, and at the height of the Vietnam War in 1968, the Army grew to over 1,570,000 men and women. The conscripted Army of the Vietnam War had a disproportionate representation of lower-income and noncollege-educated soldiers in its ranks, with many middle and upper class men able to qualify for student deferments by attending college. This perceived unfairness of the draft and the protracted nature of the Vietnam War were credited with helping to bring about the All-Volunteer Force.

In 1970, in anticipation of a drawdown in Vietnam, the Army instituted a reduction in force— known as an RIF—with the intent of getting rid of low-performing soldiers that had accumulated during Vietnam. The process was applied unevenly and, although the Army eliminated some "deadwood," a significant number of good soldiers were released and many substandard soldiers remained on active duty.

1973 was a pivotal year for the U.S. Army as direct involvement in Vietnam's ground war ended and the transition to an all-volunteer Army began. Many believed the Army was a weakened institution, and military and political leaders were blamed by many for the poor conduct and outcome of the war. Because of the unpopular nature of the war, many returning soldiers faced a hostile or indifferent public reception. Noted one historian, "[T]he Army that left Vietnam and returned to America and its garrisons in Germany and Korea in the 1970s was at low ebb on morale, discipline, and military effectiveness."

The withdrawal of U.S. forces from Vietnam in 1973 also ushered in an era of decreased defense budgets. In 1973, in light of budgetary constraints, Secretary of Defense James Schlesinger formally instituted the Total Force. These budget reductions translated into a smaller Army, and the Army's endstrength declined from its Vietnam War high of 1.57 million in FY1968 to 785,000 in FY1974. By 1974, the Army fielded 13 Active Duty divisions.

Chief of Staff of the Army General Creighton Abrams believed that a 13-division Active Duty Army was insufficient to meet the United States' global requirements. Furthermore, the Army's Director of Manpower and Forces noted the Army's 13 divisions constituted the smallest force since prior to the

Korean War and, in reality, the Army could field only 12 divisions, and only 4 of those divisions were rated as "combat ready."

General Abrams obtained the Secretary of Defense's approval to increase the Army's active divisions to 16 without an increase in Army Active Duty endstrength, which stood at 765,000. This was achieved, in part, by shifting soldiers from Army headquarters and instructional units to Army divisions, assigning reserve component "round-out" brigades to late-deploying Active Duty divisions, and moving combat support and combat service support units to the Reserve Component.

There were a number of perceived problems associated with the Total Force. Filling the Army's three new Active Duty divisions from capped endstrength severely taxed the Army's already thin manpower pool. The relationship between the Active Duty and Reserve Components was considered by many as poor, with Active Duty commanders typically viewing their Reserve Component counterparts as "weekend warriors" and doubting the combat readiness of reserve forces. The heavy reliance on reserve forces for combat support and service support also meant active forces would have a difficult time operating in the early days of a major conflict until reserve forces could be mobilized and trained up to standard. While some viewed the heavy reliance on reserve forces as problematic, General Abrams believed increased reliance on the reserves would be beneficial in obtaining American public support in the event of a major conflict and avoiding the kind of public dissonance associated with Vietnam. Issues related to limited Army endstrength versus requirements, poor recruit quality, budgetary constraints, and lack of public support in the mid-to-late 1970s led senior Army leadership to characterize the Army as being a "hollow force."

Post-Cold War/Desert Storm

The "hollow force" of the mid-1970s and early 1980s recovered due in part to the arguments of senior DOD leaders, congressional action, and the defense build-up under the Reagan Administration. In 1987, the Active Army consisted of 780,815 personnel comprising 18 divisions, with 2 of the 18 divisions still forming and not yet at 100% strength. In late 1989, the Warsaw Pact and Soviet Union began to unravel. The demise of the Soviet Union led the United States and its allies to pursue a "peace dividend," whereby defense budgets and manpower would be drastically reduced in order to decrease taxes and divert resources to other uses. In the end, a 535,000 soldier Active Duty force—a more than 30% cut—was agreed to, constituting the smallest Army since 1939.

The late 1980s saw a fundamental rethinking of U.S. defense policy and Army force structure. A 1987 Army force structure review examining the declining Soviet threat recommended a smaller force structure of 15 divisions and 640,000 soldiers. This force level and structure was referred to as the "BASE Force." Under this scenario, Chief of Staff of the Army Carl Vuono argued that decreasing force structure by more than 35,000 soldiers per year would jeopardize readiness. Many believed in order to achieve any meaningful savings, the Army would need to be smaller than General Vuono's 640,000 soldier Army. Iraq's August 1990 invasion of Kuwait suspended downsizing debates. At the conclusion of the "100 Hour War" to liberate Kuwait, many saw it as a validation of a more technologically focused approach toward warfare, and the policy debates about reducing the size of the Army were renewed.

In 1993, the Clinton Administration announced it would pursue defense budget reductions of at least $88 billion from FY1994 to FY1997. As part of this effort, Secretary of Defense Les Aspin initiated a Bottom Up Review intended to modify force structure based on current and projected threats to national security. The review recommended placing added emphasis on U.S. air power and a reduction of Army endstrength to 495,000 soldiers while retaining the ability to fight two MTWs simultaneously. In March 1994, the Bottom Up Review recommendations were implemented and Active Army endstrength reductions to 495,000 soldiers began and 2 of 12 divisions were eliminated.

End Notes

[1] Information from this section is taken from U.S. Department of Defense News Transcript, "DOD News Briefing with Secretary Gates and Admiral Mullen from the Pentagon," January 6, 2011.

[2] Information in this section is taken from U.S. Department of Defense News Transcript, "Major Budget Decisions Briefing from the Pentagon," presented by Secretary of Defense Leon E. Panetta and Chairman of the Joint Chiefs of Staff General Martin E. Dempsey, January 26, 2012; U.S. Department of Defense News Transcript, "Major Budget Decisions Briefing from the Pentagon," presented by Deputy Secretary of Defense Ashton B. Carter and Vice Chairman of the Joint Chiefs of Staff Admiral James A. Winnefeld Jr., January 26, 2012; and U.S. Department of Defense Publication, Sustaining U.S. Global Leadership: Priorities for 21st Century Defense, January 2012.

[3] According to NATO, http://www.nato.int/terrorism/five.htm, Article 5 of the Washington Treaty is the basis of a fundamental principle of the North Atlantic Treaty Organization. It provides that if a NATO Ally is the victim of an armed attack, each and every other member of the Alliance will consider this act of violence as an armed attack against all members and will take the actions it deems necessary to assist the Ally attacked. This is the principle of collective defense.

[4] According to NATO, http://www.nato.int/cps/en/natolive/topics_49755.htm, The NATO Response Force (NRF) is a highly ready and technologically advanced multinational force made up of land, air, maritime, and special forces components that the Alliance can deploy quickly to wherever it is needed. It is comprised of three parts: a command and control element from the NATO Command Structure; the Immediate Response Force, a joint force of about 13,000 high-readiness troops provided by Allies; and a Response Forces Pool, which can supplement the Immediate Response Force when necessary.

[5] Information in this section is taken from DOD White Paper "Defense Budget Priorities and Choices," January 2012 and transcripts of Army Chief of Staff Raymond T. Odierno Army Briefing on the FY-13 Budget Request, January 27, 2012.

[6] Transcripts of Army Chief of Staff Raymond T. Odierno, Army Briefing on the FY-13 Budget Request, January 27, 2012.

[7] Ibid.

[8] Ibid.

[9] Armored BCTs were formerly known as Heavy BCTs (HBCTs).

[10] Army Information Paper, "Subject: Army Force Structure in Europe," February 16, 2012.

[11] Ibid.

[12] Information in this section is taken from Sebastian Sprenger, "Odierno: Army May Cut More Than Eight Brigade Combat Teams," InsideDefense.com, January 27, 2012; Michelle Tan and Richard Sandza, "European Pullout: Plan to Move 2 BCTs and Up to 10,000 Soldiers Could Start in October," Army Times, January 23, 2012; and Michelle Tan, "Reduction to Include 8 BCTs," Army Times, February 6, 2012.

[13] "USAREUR to Cut Civilian Jobs," Army Times, November 30, 2012.

[14] William Cole, "Army Won't Shrink Force Level in Pacific Region, General Says," Honolulu Star-Advertiser, January 18, 2102.

[15] Information in this section is taken from DOD White Paper "Defense Budget Priorities and Choices," January 2012 and transcripts of Army Chief of Staff Raymond T. Odierno Army Briefing on the FY-13 Budget Request, January 27, 2012.

[16] Sebastian Sprenger, "Odierno: Army May Cut More Than Eight Brigade Combat Teams," InsideDefense.com, January 27, 2012.

[17] Information in this section is taken from U.S. Department of Defense News Transcript, "Major Budget Decisions Briefing from the Pentagon," presented by Secretary of Defense Leon E. Panetta and Chairman of the Joints Chiefs of Staff General Martin E. Dempsey, January 26, 2012; U.S. Department of Defense News Transcript, "Major Budget Decisions Briefing from the Pentagon," presented by Deputy Secretary of Defense Ashton B. Carter and Vice Chairman of the Joint Chiefs of Staff Admiral James A. Winnefeld Jr., January 26, 2012; and U.S. Department of Defense Publication, Sustaining U.S. Global Leadership: Priorities for 21st Century Defense, January 2012.

[18] Ibid.

[19] Information in this section is taken from Lolita C. Baldor, "Army Chief Sees Greater Role for Guard and Reserves," Norfolk Virginian-Pilot, January 27, 2012.

[20] Transcripts of Army Chief of Staff Raymond T. Odierno, Army Briefing on the FY-13 Budget Request, January 27, 2012.

[21] U.S. Department of Defense News Release, "DOD Announces U.S. Army in Europe Force Structure Changes," No. 120-13, March 1, 2013.

[22] Information in this section is taken from Army Information Paper for Members of Congress, "Army Force Structure and Stationing," June 25, 2013 and Army Public Affairs Guidance on Army Force Structure and Stationing Decisions, June 24, 2013.

[23] Army Information Paper for Members of Congress, "Army Force Structure and Stationing," June 25, 2013.

[24] Michelle Tan, "Army Accelerates BCT Overhaul by Two Years," Army Times, October 21, 2013.

[25] Ibid. Article attributes this quote from Col. Daniel King, a spokesman for Army Forces Command (FORSCOM).

[26] Information in this section is taken from Jim Tice, "High-Speed Drawdown: Army Ramps Up Force-Outs," Army Times, October 21, 2013.

[27] Ibid.

[28] Michelle Tan, "Army Accelerates BCT Overhaul by Two Years," Army Times, October 21, 2013.

[29] Ibid.

[30] Paul McLeary and Michelle Tan, "A 25 Percent Cut for HQs," Army Times, September 2, 2013.

[31] Tony Bertuca, "Odierno: 85 Percent of Army BCTs Will be Unprepared if Sequester Stays Put," InsideDefense.com, September 20, 2013.

[32] For a complete description of the Stop Loss program, see CRS Report R40121, U.S. Military Stop Loss Program: Key Questions and Answers.

[33] Military Review, "Saving Military Families," by Captain (Navy) Gene Thomas Gomulka, January-February 2010.

[34] Department of Defense, "Overview: Fiscal Year 2013 Budget Request," Office of the Under Secretary of Defense (Comptroller), February 2012.

[35] The FY2013 Budget also announced a drawdown for the Marine Corps from its current strength of 202,100 to 182,100, also by FY2017.

[36] §540, P.L. 110-417, October 14, 2008. Congress expanded each of the service academy programs—U.S. Military Academy, U.S. Naval Academy and the U.S. Air Force Academy from 4,000 to 4,400 as determined for any year as of the day before the last day of the academic year.

[37] Department of the Army Message, Selected Early Retirement Board dated March 22, 2013 and Jen Judson, "Army Plans to Involuntarily Retire Excess Colonels, Lieutenant Colonels," InsideDefense.com, April 3, 2013.

[38] Information in this section is taken from Sebastian Sprenger, "Leaders Envision Institutional Army as Buffer Against Loss of Talent," InsideDefense.com, November 12, 2012.

[39] Andrew Tilghman, "Advisory Board to Suggest Military Heavy on Reserves," Army Times, September 9, 2013.

[40] Ibid.

[41] For a detailed discussion of each drawdown authority, see David McCormick's "The Downsized Warrior: America's Army in Transition," 1998.

[42] §638, Title 10.

[43] §647, Title 10.

[44] Information in this section is taken from Army Message dated 141359Z March 2012, Subject: Enlisted Qualitative Service Program (QSP).

[45] Calculating the actual value of any of these voluntary programs requires individual calculations best done by a finance and accounting professional.

[46] §504, P.L. 112-81, December 31, 2011.

[47] §1175, Title 10.

[48] P.L. 102-190, December 5, 1991.

[49] §504, P.L. 112-81, December 31, 2011.

[50] §1174a, Title 10.

[51] §504, P.L. 112-81, December 31, 2011.

[52] §1293, Title 10 (note).

[53] §647, Title 10.

[54] §1171, Title 10.

[55] §525, P.L. 112-81, December 31, 2011.

[56] The Wall Street Journal, "Air Force Is Following Congress's Mandate, as It Must," January 6, 2012.

In: Force Reduction
Editor: Geoffrey Hopkins

Chapter 3

OP-ED: DOWNSIZING THE ARMY PROFESSION[*]

Dr. Leonard Wong

John Carpenter, film director of horror movies such as *Halloween*, was once asked what he thought it was that scared theater audiences the most. His answer was simple: "Uncertainty." Carpenter understood that not knowing what will happen next often produces more anxiety and angst than actual traumatic events. As anyone who has sat on the edge of their chair during thrillers such as *Psycho* or *Jaws* understands, it's the apprehension and dread resulting from uncertainty that exacts the most psychological toll from viewers.

Unfortunately, today's Army finds itself reading from a script saturated with uncertainty. For a force accustomed to the draining yet preordained forecasts of the "Patch Chart" and the frenetic yet predictable pace of the ARFORGEN cycle, the end of the war in Afghanistan signals the beginning of a journey into the unknown. Soldiers—many of whom have known nothing but the *Groundhog Day* routine of deploying or preparing to deploy—now find themselves in an Army with undefined budgetary conditions and a still evolving mission.

Looming large over the entire situation, however, is the specter of the Army's impending downsizing driven by the curtailed demand for troops in

---

[*] This is an edited, reformatted and augmented version of an article published by the Strategic Studies Institute on May 8, 2013.

Afghanistan and accelerated by a nation anxious to spend its treasure on more pressing domestic concerns. The inevitable downsizing will result in the reduction of the active duty rolls from an Army of 570,000 to a force of 490,000 (or less, according to murmurings in the blogosphere) by the end of fiscal year 2017.

Of course, the Army has already been down this path many times before, so executing a downsizing should almost be routine by now. For example, the Army's active duty end strength after the Vietnam War dropped from 1.5 million to about 780,000 in a little over 5 years. But that force reduction included the momentous shift from a conscripted force to an all-volunteer Army. And one would be hard pressed to find anyone who would claim that the post-Vietnam downsizing—typified by insensitive dismissals of combat veterans via pink slips accompanied by almost nonexistent transition assistance—is an example of a well-executed reduction in force.

With the fall of the Berlin Wall and the end of the Cold War, the Army once again reduced its size during the early 1990s, going from 780,000 soldiers to 480,000. During that downsizing, the Army deliberately endeavored to avoid the pitfalls and blunders of the post-Vietnam force reductions. For example, instead of summarily dismissing officers, the Army expended significant energy minimizing the use of involuntary separation programs, while heavily promoting a variety of more compassionate (and expensive) voluntary separation options. Additionally, the Army took great pains to provide assistance to those transitioning out of the force by fielding programs offering job placement and career counseling.

While the post-Cold War downsizing served to exorcise many of the demons of the painful post-Vietnam experience, it should be noted that the cutbacks of the 1990s were executed in an environment much different than today's situation. For example, in 1995 the unemployment rate was 5.5% compared to a 7.7% jobless rate today. Additionally, with the once-thought-impossible sequester now a reality, the probability of additional, and even deeper, cuts in defense spending seems not so unlikely. Across the world, incidents in Iraq and Afghanistan reveal that global unrest continues to simmer, while tensions involving North Korea, Iran, and Syria add to worldwide instability. In other words, the current downsizing will be implemented in a much more acutely unsure and uncertain environment.

In such a time of flux and volatility, it is imperative that the Army redouble its efforts to diminish the uncertainty associated with the downsizing. To be sure, much of the uncertainty originates from decisions (or indecision) outside the Army and is therefore inevitable and unavoidable. Nevertheless, there are some overarching principles that can guide the Army's efforts in minimizing the impact of uncertainty during the force reduction.

First, the Army must publish its downsizing plan as soon as possible to include specifying target reduction numbers, as well as describing the programs designed to entice, encourage, or compel Soldiers to leave the service. A detailed plan allows those who desire to stay to know when the risk of being downsized has passed, and it gives those who are thinking of leaving an improved ability to assess their options. More importantly, a thorough and transparent plan shows the entire force that the Army is engaged, proactive, and rational despite the fog of uncertainty surrounding the downsizing.

Second—and this is particularly crucial for the officer corps—the Army must identify those who are at risk and those who are the top talent. For too long, perfunctory promotion boards and inflated performance appraisals have conveyed the impression that every officer is above average. In these days, the Army must be brutally honest in communicating to officers where they stand in relation to their peers. No involuntarily separated officer should say that they were not warned that they were at risk for separation. Likewise, the Army should identify and doggedly pursue the most talented officers for retention. Note that the process of ensuring that each officer is aware of their relative position in their cohort can occur before the final downsizing plan is in place.

Third, as Defense Secretary Chuck Hagel recently pointed out, the downsizing is not only an occasion to understand the challenges and uncertainties associated with a reduction in force, but to also recognize the opportunities inherent in budget constraints. In other words, if the Army is going to rebalance to the Asia-Pacific theater, bolster cyber warfare capabilities, or strive to produce more strategically thinking senior leaders, then the downsizing is an opportune time to adjust force structure and shape the Army's talent toward those ends. In other words, the downsizing is more than just shrinking the size of the Army. It is also a chance to thoughtfully reestablish priorities and judiciously refocus now limited resources.

Finally, the downsizing must result from the concerted efforts of both the Army bureaucracy and the Army profession. The Army bureaucracy will efficiently reduce the Army's financial footprint while maintaining adequate levels of combat readiness. It is the Army bureaucracy that will carefully balance end strength and force structure within directed fiscal constraints. Additionally, it is the Army bureaucracy that will devise the myriad programs to eventually execute the force reductions.

However, it is the Army profession that will ensure that downsizing programs are carried out with meticulous care and compassion. It is the Army profession that will rally around those encouraged or induced to leave—including their families—and offer generous assistance in the transition to civilian life. It will also be the Army profession that clearly understands that the manner in which the Army conducts the downsizing will affect not only those who leave, but also those who remain; American society will also be curious to see if the Army really never leaves a fallen comrade behind.

The Army has made great strides reestablishing itself as a profession during a decade of war. Ultimately, the swirling uncertainty surrounding the downsizing can only be mitigated by, once again, the Army profession taking care of its own, thus continuing to earn the trust of both its Soldiers and the society it serves.

***

(About the Author: Leonard Wong is a research professor in the Strategic Studies Institute at the U.S. Army War College who focuses on the human and organizational dimensions of the military. He is a retired lieutenant colonel whose career includes teaching leadership at West Point and serving as an analyst for the Chief of Staff of the Army.)

INDEX